Lizbe

Let's Talk About It

Por La Buena
O La Mala

Illustrations by Jamcy Stephen Maquilon

Charleston, SC
www.PalmettoPublishing.com

Let's Talk About It

Copyright © 2020 by Lizbel Ortiz

Hardcover ISBN: 978-1-64990-293-1
Paperback ISBN: 978-1-64111-949-8
eBook ISBN: 978-1-64990-022-7

To my family
Every argument that led to understanding,
Every tear met with compassion,
Every disagreement that ended in forgiveness,
Every joke that ended in us gasping for air,
Have led us to this exact moment.
The greatest things about me, came from you.
Different branches to the same tree.
Planted solid, so we all move freely -
At the root is an unshakable foundation.
Prayers from decades ago still protecting us.
May we cherish it,
May we protect it,
May we teach it.
Legacy.

Table Of Contents

Acknowledgments

A small woman with a big spirit. I have questioned many things in this short life, but my Mother's love has never been one of them. We have uncovered wounds and healed ourselves through hard, internal, vulnerable work. I always say that I have walked through fire to be where I am today, but you have held my hand the entire time. Every moment where you quietly brought me sliced fruits, I knew a love like this did not exist outside of you. I would need 1,000 extra lives to be able to repay you for everything you have done for me. You are my world, la Reina.

To my dad who always taught me there are two things you should always stand by: your code of ethics and your family. He taught us to split everything four ways and if you couldn't, give it away. A constant teacher who never let me mispronounce any word in any language, you are partly the reason I am on a constant learning journey today. I love you in this lifetime and the next.

To my mother's other three, strange-faced children, who while growing up dealt with my ideas and thoughts before I learned how to communicate them: I love you beyond words.

Firstly, to Irisbelle: you are the soul mate God knew I needed. You have shown me how to build myself back from the ground up and, most importantly, to laugh loudly... at everything. My first best friend, my first test of patience, my first roommate, my only sister. You are the Mary J to my Lil Kim. You taught me how to stand up for myself and how to ask for what I want. Your laugh brings joy to this world and it fills our rooms with life. I hope you know that no matter where my two feet land on this green earth, I take your wise words with me everywhere I go… *"Bitch, get it together."*

To my big brother, Andy: calling you my best friend would be an understatement. I always joked that we were twins, but I took an extra year to cook up so I stayed behind, explaining why I am smarter and better looking. You have helped me overcome fears I did not know existed in me, and you have heard every polished and edited chapter in this book but in an unfiltered, vicious fueled car rant. You have seen me at my worst and made me feel like I was still the best, all while still holding me accountable. You are the master of light and you bring it everywhere you go. I would never be able to repay you for what you have gifted me in this lifetime. So many of our days are spent laughing hysterically but even when moments are bad, you know how to cover us in comfort and sit in silence. You make everything better.

To my little brother, Elvin: writing this book would not have been as easy as it was without you practicing your guitar in the next room and serenading me while I wrote. You are one of the most creative and talented people I know and having someone like you in my life keeps me on my toes. I hope you know how much having you in our lives has made us all so much better. Our bond is something only we understand, that is what makes it so special. You are the funniest and strangest encounter I have ever had in my life.

To Tausee: we spent our teenage years sitting on my stoop talking about everything under the sun. We questioned all things our parents, schools, religion, and the world taught us. We laughed, cried, and fought, but most importantly, we grew. As adults, our bond became peeling back layers of our lives on how to heal and develop a plan to move our people forward in all ways. You are a selfless man who has mastered the art in helping your people in more ways than one. You have taught me so much and you were truly specifically put into my life for so many reasons. Our friendship was formed by God himself. The F is for Forever.

To Nelson: your mind should be put in a museum. A soul like yours comes once in a lifetime and I do not say that lightly. You were a vital component in one of the biggest breakthroughs of my life and helped me release some of my most gripping fears that eventually led to me finally mustering up the courage to publish this book. God knew how much I needed someone like you in my life. You are a visionary, a genius, an artist and a leader, but more than anything you are an amazing man. I am honored to have a front row seat at your greatness. I love you, 3000.

Carlos, your loyalty and friendship are unmatched. You have only brought laughter, love and selflessness into my life since I have met you. As an adult, I see a friend like you truly comes once in a lifetime. Thank you for allowing me to experience your humor, gentle, kind and beautiful spirit in this lifetime. You are one in a million.

Jodie, you have been the closest thing to a second sister since I was 15 years old. We have laughed until we cried, cried until we laughed, fought, loved, and fought again. We learned many of the troubles of this life together and so much of these topics were discussed as teenagers learning to navigate this weird ass world. This could not have happened without you.

Jaribel, I do not know how to verbally express the love you ooze from your pores, but I am honored to have you in my life. You are a beam of beauty in this dark world. If it were not for you and Jodie putting the bug in my ear, this book probably would not have happened for a very long time. Our bond feels like home. I love you, forever.

To the ones who have redirected me to my path when I drifted off, thank you for believing in me.

This one is for us.

In honor of Lenny and Webbie.

Men who were too courageous,
Too powerful,
And too magical for this world.
Putting your body on the line to help others,
Is the ultimate show of character.
You are the heroes they make movies about.
It was an honor to experience you.
I hope I have made you proud.
I love you forever.

Introduction

I am the youngest of three children born to parents who immigrated to this country from the Dominican Republic in the 1980s. They moved to a foreign land with no money or experience and a different native tongue, but still my mom and dad began to build a life in Brooklyn, New York with whatever lessons and knowledge they had brought back from the island. I grew up on Atkins and Belmont, in a neighborhood that was a mixture of cultures, a home to many Immigrants from the Dominican Republic, Jamaica, Trinidad, Cuba and Haiti. The kind of home where your next door neighbor would feed your sons on the days your mom worked late. The kind of home where Primo from the Bodega let you grab a free icee or water on a lucky summer day. The kind of home where we nervously knocked on each others doors to ask parents to let their kids come out and play. Our block parties were all day events we had to physically prepare for. This was the kind of home that showed bonds and strength through struggle. A community with languages as borders that leaned on each other and communicated through love. My mom birthed three children but raised four, all while working on foreign land. As children, you do not understand what poverty or lack of money is. Of course, eventually you catch on to the things you would not be able to do or buy as you get older, but for the most part, you remember how you felt. For me, I did not care about the price of my Sketchers; I was just happy my dad remembered to get my favorite color. My father was a cab driver, like most Dominican dads who spend their nights picking up passengers and using their steering wheels as drums to the beat of old school Bachata. As a child, cabbing around New York City with him were some of my favorite moments as we spent the time laughing and singing, with him talking to me about the old times. He was a teacher back at home, who taught English, Spanish, and French on his island. This was a gift and a curse, as he never let me mispronounce a word in any language, no matter how many times he made me repeat it. He spent a lot of his time teaching me random facts and history lessons about the world and the small things that make this world what it is. This is partially the reason why I love to learn new things so much today.

My mom was a caregiver, who spent her evenings looking after the elderly and young children with disabled parents. On the weekends, she volunteered her time to churches and prayer groups. She had a passion for helping: it did not matter who. I did not realize until I turned about 13 that I was having a completely different experience than the other kids I went to school with. To be a first generation American is to have your entire life on a collapsing bridge between the United States and your ancestral country—a constant battle between wanting to build and represent for your people here or running back to your true home to help. I did not realize until I was older that I was the arm that connected the two. I spent many of my teenage years having intense conversations regarding various taboo subjects with family and friends. Many of these conversations ranged from pedophiles in our churches to violent sexists in our homes. I spent many years uncovering wounds that led to dark places. We spoke of trauma so deep many of us did not know it was even there. After years of internal work and being vulnerable and honest with myself, life seems brighter. As hard as it is to sit in silence with yourself and admit your faults, it is also one of the most rewarding experiences. At first, it will feel violent: you will feel sad, angry, resentful, prideful, and completely under attack. You will want to run from it, but I hope you run *to* it. The peace that comes with processing and healing yourself is special because it is a gift only you can give yourself. After years of learning, reading, and researching the many things that held me back throughout the years, I simply wished I had known all of it sooner. God has a funny way of leading you into your destiny. I wrote this book because I wanted to give others a head start. In my short years of living, I never thought I would be an author; I only knew that I had a restless feeling all of my life. As if I had so much to say and was screaming internally but was never able to get it out… until now.

This book was written with minorities and young women in mind. I wanted to bring light to the conversations we had in our living rooms, hair salons, churches, and barbershops, the ones we whisper and argue about in privacy then act as if it doesn't exist in public. I felt it was time to uncover these taboo issues that hurt our communities so we can heal collectively, much faster. I do not know if you bought this book, or if someone passed it along as a gift. Whichever way it landed into your palm, I want to say thank you. While I wrote this book for all minorities in mind, right now it is just you and me. Throughout your journey of reading this book, I ask of you only one thing: let your guard down. Allow yourself to be as honest and vulnerable as you can throughout it as it was written with the intention of healing, helping, and honoring us. I hope you learn, laugh, cry or get upset. If it makes you feel anything, I have done my part. If you get defensive, upset or hurt, I want you to peel back the layers of why you feel this way. This book is meant for healing hurt in so many ways and it requires honesty and self-awareness that can sometimes hurt to acknowledge. While I started writing this book when I was 21, I did not complete it until I was 26. It makes me wonder what takes you longer—the actual process of your art or building up enough confidence to release it to the world? I have treated this book as my baby. I wrote so much my fingers cramped, thought so much my mind collapsed, read so much my eyes gave out. Yet still, the hardest part of it all was removing the layers of my ego so I could give to you my most vulnerable creation yet.

I have always loved reading and learning, as the information in this world is endless, but I have always been my own filter—listening and dissecting what I needed for my life and what I would discard. I will treat this book no differently.

Take what you need,

Leave what you don't.

Pass on what will help others.

I hope this heals you in ways it did for me.

Let's talk about it.

CHAPTER 1
In the Eyes of the Church:
Los Tiempos de Antes

M y grandmother is a woman of very few words: an introvert, a people watcher, and an incredible listener. She sits in her corner everywhere we go, watching how people move, what they say, and how they say it; in ten minutes she will be ready to go home. I see very easily where I get my personality. She does not speak much in public, so when it's just the two of us, I hang on to every word. She was 16 when her parents decided whom she would be spending the rest of her life with. She was born in 1935, a time when arranged marriages were common and were based on the relationship of the four parents and not on the two who were getting married. In most of these countries, as long as you fit into the mold of a girl who would be a good mother or a boy who was hard working, they will find you somebody to "begin" your life with. Except that in the Dominican Republic, the boys learn to work before they learn to breathe and girls become moms the second they learn to walk, as many of them have been taking care of their sisters and brothers since they were born. My grandparents knew nothing of each other. She had no idea if he was a serial killer or if he preferred "Friends" over "Martin." I know these did not exist, but my point is there are people you simply cannot trust. My grandfather's and her fate had been decided for them, and it was important for the marriage to be traditional, which consisted of him going out to provide food and shelter while Mama had the children and kept the home.

They went on to have eight children and have accumulated a countless number of grandchildren and great-grandchildren. We honored the legacy they had built and celebrated their 62-year anniversary in one of the most beautiful ceremonies my family had ever had. Watching this relationship since childhood had been one of my highest honors and biggest blessings. They laid an incredible foundation that instilled unity, love, and respect into us all. We spent every Sunday at their home and spent all major and minor holidays there, looking for any excuse for us all to get together. This did not mean we did not suffer; it just means we worked really hard to prioritize the good over the bad, and we leaned on each other in the worst times. Papa was a firecracker, an old man with child-like energy and a laugh so contagious it did not matter if you were having the worst day of your life. Mama is an incredibly peaceful and calm-spirited woman, an introverted woman who stands on her faith and family. While we are so much alike, I inherited the fire she internalized. Growing up as a teenager, I spent my Sundays going up against the patriarchs of our family: men who have never had a woman, let alone a little girl, talk back to them. I questioned traditions, morals, racist and sexist double standards, and the lack of accountability in our culture. In so many instances, in the midst of my going back and forth, I would glance over to see Mama in her corner—watching, listening, and smiling at me in silence. I understand the privilege it is to be able to talk to power and not be silenced. I do not take it for granted and give all the credit to the women who fought for me.

While other women rushed me to get married, my grandparents always told me to take my time; as they knew what it was like to not have choices. Mama told me marriage was a joining of two people with different backgrounds, but the most important thing they had in common was their love and respect for one another. Before, women were not allowed to lead their own lives and were always to be represented by a male figure, especially if they were in public. This representation could have been your father, brother, husband, or eventually your son. Women were not allowed to work, go to school, or read. Men controlled what went on in the home and were in charge of the laws that prohibited women from advancing financially and because men were perceived as more intelligent, stronger, and harder workers; this made them the head of the house and kept women at home. Our churches and Bibles pushed the notion of women submitting to their husbands, while women who denied this were considered to be witches or lesbians. In my church they taught us that marriage was basically a bid. It was something you could never get out of because to get a divorce is to commit ultimate sin. For some, this ties them into a life of unity with two different individuals who are jointed in one common mission. It means to have a solid foundation of love, honesty, and respect for each other that is so deep nobody, not even death itself, can separate you. For some, this meant dealing with years of manipulation, violence, and abuse in the name of a "good marriage." This meant dealing with abusive alcoholics and drug addicts, infidelity that led to children outside of their marriages, and years of anxiety, depression, and self-doubt due to decades of manipulation and abuse. Men were under-developed as fathers since housework and caregiving were considered women's jobs; they did not know the difference between being an active father and a provider. We just knew they lived with us, paid for the food on the table, and scared the living shit out of us when we did not follow the rules. So while our parents enjoyed telling us *"ustedes no saben nada de eso"* ("you young kids don't know anything about that.") every time they talked about the old times, I for one would like to agree.

While it is true that they say Millennials have tossed out many traditional values, I will say we have gotten rid of very damaging ones too. You no longer have to physically stay in places due to lack of resources. We notice that the most successful marriages are with those who see each other as equals and have no boundaries as to what can or cannot be done for each other. We understand that gender does not limit you to housework, care giving, or being able to provide financially. These changes have led to women building stable and strong careers for themselves, finding their power in their creativity, and taking care of themselves financially. It has meant breaking the shackles of not being able to provide for yourself and sitting in abuse because by law you had to. This change has also allowed men to be incredibly more active as fathers and become emotionally invested in raising their children and not just being paycheck providers and the enforcers of rules. More than ever, new dads are forming incredible bonds with the little people they created and are not as distant and emotionally abusive as historically many fathers have been. Women have been given the space to lead their lives, and men have been given the space to become emotionally intelligent without our femininity or masculinity being questioned. This is not to say traditional marriages don't work, because that would be incredibly false. It means that it should never be mandatory. There are many young people who still follow these traditional values, and it has worked for their family dynamics. You are not a weak woman if you follow these traditions, take his last name, or are a stay-at-home mom. If this is what you wanted in your heart, you are just as powerful as the woman who decided to keep her name or build a legacy through her company. It is the power of choice.

My mom showed me this first hand as a caretaker and incredibly hard worker. After every fall and scratch or mishap in my life, I could count on this superwoman to be there. She had worked every job under the sun.

She flipped burgers at the King, took care of a family of 12, and still had time to make it home every night to take care of her children, husband, and parents. I see now she was not a superwoman but a woman with a lot on her plate, who was simply trying to keep her head above water. It took my becoming a woman to step outside of my shoes and look at my mother as just that. Another woman. Not the woman who birthed me or who I thought she was, but who she was before her children and marriage. How did she navigate her life when I was not here? Why is she the way she is? What has she been through? What traumas did she endure? What has she suffered in silence about? What does she believe about herself? Does she have insecurities? What about doubts? Does she question her capabilities? Does she believe she is a bad mom? Have I ever made her feel like she was? I went down this list of questions and could not help but have a revelation on how I had treated her as purely my caregiver and not a woman who had been healing herself just like me.

My mom is 5'2" with hands of steel; she married my father when she was 20 but never changed her last name, which in that time would make you liable to be burned at the stake. I remember as a kid always watching her fill out documents and sign her name across the line that was different than mine. When I was about 11, I finally mustered up the courage to ask her why we all had the same last name and she did not. By the fast head turn and the glisten in her eyes, you could tell she was surprised by the question. With a slight grin she stated six words that would change the trajectory of my life forever... *"Porque no me dio la gana."* Wow. She did not do it simply because she did not want to. I could have sworn I heard a glass shatter, but it was most likely my years of exaggerated Telenovela senses triggering up again. It was the first time in my short-lived life I had seen a woman reject something, simply because she wanted to. She went on to tell me how important her name was to her life and legacy, how it was something given to her at birth, and was something she wanted to keep intact until the day she departs. I do not know if she knew it then, but at that moment my life changed. I realized I had choices, and that what was presented to me was just that—an option. That I did not have to choose only what was shown to me. I spent most of my teenage years and still until this day being referred to as *"una malcriada"* a feisty and disrespectful young girl who had far too much to say. I have been referred to all kinds of words used to silence powerful women simply because I did not allow myself to be used as a doormat, and nobody was going to beat my ass about it. Later in life, I looked back and saw the fire my grandmother said was burning inside of me that had been lit by my mother. I understand I am only one woman and that breaking generational curses is not for the weak, but if you're reading this, it means there are two of us. The signs are everywhere. Use the strength and honor given to us by the ones who came before us.

CHAPTER 2
Sexually Transmitted Demons:
Prolonging Trauma

In this new age you have a perfect blend of childhood insecurities and unresolved issues that are elevated by the pressures of society and social media. Later on this becomes a combination of two sexually transmitted demons uniting into a nonprofit relationship with anybody who will tolerate them. There are so many relationships built on people who realistically do not like each other or have dated for years on shaky foundations so time has just been passing by with them being seat fillers. When two children, who have been incredibly hurt, grow up to be adults who are still denying or processing these issues, end up together, chaos with a little extra sugar is the final recipe. Unfortunately, many of us did not grow up in perfect homes with emotionally intelligent and developed people. Sixty-two percent of humans have deeply hidden childhood traumas, which means sixty-two percent of the world's population can be living their entire lives projecting and re-creating chaos because they still see the world according to what they once suffered as children. This can happen especially if these things go unattended for years and can hurt every important dynamic in your life, plus ruin any form of connection with friends, family, and present or future romantic partners.

Now this chapter is for those who have situations that stem so far your memory can barely reach it. All you can remember is the pain you felt and the changes in you that came after. So much so that your brain begins what is called blocking. Sometimes, if you had a traumatic childhood, you can lose a lot of memories from that particular time as our brain reacts as a defense mechanism when you avoid tragedy and cannot accept or process what has happened. Some of these things stem so deep your mind has buried them, literally. By the time you reach the root you realize it is the main factor determining why you are the way you are and why you behave the way you do. These unresolved traumas can trickle down into our relationships, careers, children, and ultimately our peace of mind. They are thieves of joy and find holes in every inch of your happiness. A lot of painful things like being humiliated by those you love, being abused sexually, mentally, verbally, or physically, being raised by people who were alcoholics, experiencing or witnessing domestic violence and drug abuse, suddenly losing someone you love to death, prison, or immigration laws, or if you were raised in a family that did not show love, unity, or affection. Some of the side effects that can stick with you after years have passed are lacking social skills, being infatuated with isolation, and avoiding closeness or intimacy with others, seeing abuse as a true form of love and denying yourself happiness because of your lack of self-worth. Many people who have gone through tough things believe they are far too damaged to be loved and would rather not put people through the heartache. Some of these people can confuse themselves by being an introvert, but they are further from the truth. Introverts get their energy from within, but still seek intimate close relationships even in small dosages or small groups. However, someone who is hurting does not believe in getting close at all; they avoid all forms of happiness because they think it leads to disappointment. There are countless men and women who are under-developed emotionally and spend a lot of their lives protecting their inner child by guarding their insecurities. You don't need to be hard on yourself, and if you have built a wall around yourself due to the things you have been through as a child, I, for one, am proud of you. If nobody else was there to protect you as a child, you made sure you did. You did whatever you needed to do to make sure you were safe until you finally were—and now you are.

The beauty of life is we can grow, but sometimes we keep the same habits although we are not in the same situations. When you realize that the walls you needed around you when you were ten have been keeping beautiful things and people out of your life all of this time, you can soon begin to let your guard down. These traumas literally store in your body and progress throughout the years and may eventually get you physically sick from heart disease and auto-immune disorders. When this is all we see as kids, we can become attracted to unhealthy relationships and negative situations. When a manipulator or abuser raises you, your brain rewires according to how you are being treated so you believe everyone you come across maneuvers this way. You are even dumbfounded and confused when people treat you with respect and decency. Some people grow up and meet somebody who treats them just as badly; they stay in these kinds of relationships because they are used to this form of love and it feels familiar. After years, if left unattended, these moments can lead to self-esteem issues, crippling anxiety, addiction, depression, control issues, destructiveness, and being mentally, sexually, physically, and verbally abusive to those around you.

Many times, for women, our mind loves to hold on to the parts that used to be great; this is usually what keeps us beating a dead horse and holding onto rotten relationships. We crave the memories of what once were and we create visuals in our heads of what the future could be with if this person became what you needed them to be. *Do not allow your mind to take you places your body will never go.* If there is one thing women can take away from men, it is selfishness, the good kind. The kind that makes you put yourself, your dreams, wants and your aspirations first. It does not mean you are anti-love; it means you build a life of happiness and joy outside of people so that your joy is yours and nobody can take or replace it—they can only add to it. This is important so that when you do meet someone worth bringing into your space, they become a part of your journey and not your entire story. We spend our time never experiencing or creating happiness, but waiting for someone else to come along and magically bring it to us. This is far too much pressure and power to give to somebody who is most likely still finding their own way. In some ways, women can have it all together and become consumed in relationships, forgetting about their goals, dreams, friends, and family. We are taught to believe that the more pain and mistreatment we can endure, the stronger and more solid we are, but realistically, there are a lot of women in relationships with single men. The women who are so infatuated with fairy tales that they create dreams in their heads. They stay with men who do not love or respect them. Time and time again they show you how they feel about you and what they are willing to offer. When somebody tells you they are not looking for the exact thing you *are* looking for, this should be the end of the race and not a challenge you take on. Instead of leaving, many women begin their performance of what they think he might like; they spend months over-extending themselves and doing out of the ordinary things to make this person see them as what they truly are. They believe this can change them, and I can guarantee you that it will not. Obviously, they will not say this because they are enjoying the perks of somebody giving their all without doing it in return. It is important to take what people show you at face value so you can take control of your life. If you begin a life of performing for relationships because you want to have a ring on your finger, you will first lose confidence in yourself because you are not being authentic. You are also dealing with somebody who does not love you fully, so you can begin to lose yourself in this process of trying to prove to them you are worth it. You spent five years waiting for a caterpillar to turn into a butterfly until you looked closely and saw it was a maggot. You must be able to create boundaries and, more importantly, enforce them in order to live an emotionally healthy life. Some people will see your boundaries and run while some people will stay and test the waters to see how true you are to yourself. Some will be honest and tell you they are not going to respect the boundaries, so just understand that what you accept will continue. At one point you will need to take accountability if you have allowed this and will continue to allow it. Manipulators manipulate. Liars lie. Takers take and Bitches leave. So, when people show you time and time again the pain they will keep bringing into your life, know that the only control you have is over what to do next. If there is one thing we know, it is that this world can be full of bloodsuckers, so as a man or woman who gives freely, you need to make sure that who you are giving to is not a leech. Of course, it is a lot easier said than done because so many things like our history, connections, sex, and much deeper things are tied into it. Memories, feelings, and thoughts can be incredibly hard to get rid of, but you must always remember to choose yourself over the warmth of somebody who does not love you. None of this needs an explanation. You can accept these things if you want to, but you must keep in mind that sometimes people change and sometimes people are pressing your boundaries to see how serious you are about them. You can cry on the ride or remove yourself from the circus. I have always believed that in relationships, may they be romantic, friendships, or family oriented, you are always dealing with the battle of personalities—people who have completely different upbringings, teachings, and morals and are in relationships together. There is always a tug of war between two personalities and souls. Sometimes you meet people who are amazing, but may have a tainted, negative view of the world and everything good in it. They can be mean spirited, controlling, and manipulative. The more time you spend with people, the more you adapt and get used to their way of being so you may develop some of the same habits. You could begin accepting things that you probably would have never done before, or you start doing and saying things that are not like yourself. Then there are some people you meet who have healing and happy energy, making you look at the world in a much brighter way. They make you a better person in their teachings and in the way they love, protect, and encourage you. When two completely different people come together, there will always be a tug of war and one will always win. The person who has a negative view on life can overpower the other's healing energy so he or she becomes just as mean spirited. Sometimes, however, healing personalities are so strong they can consume you and turn you into a better person.

For men, these same issues can become burdens that hover over them every single waking moment. Since most men have not been taught how to deal with their emotions accordingly, they live a very mentally chaotic life. They believe putting everything to the back of their heads is what works, and they do not give themselves the option to uncover and heal from traumas they never understood. Most men who were molested or raped did not even know it happened until they became much older. They knew something was wrong, but if they spoke about it, they became the laughing stock. Boys raised in silence can become men who would rather live in years of misery out of fear of confrontation or ridicule. Although they are suppressing most of their feelings and emotions, they can become extremely insecure, angry, and distrustful. The pressure of being somebody's entire fountain of happiness in a relationship can become draining. You take everything with a grain of salt, and you believe you are cool, calm, and collected, but most of the time you are being dismissive of your feelings and prolonging issues by not tackling them head on. These men can go on to be in relationships for years with partners who are controlling and physically abusive. They end up with people who only take from them and deal with people who will drain them. I know many fellas who have internalized verbal abuse that has left them a lifetime of wounds. I do not want men to continue dying before their time due to years of pressure from never addressing trauma and pain. There is no amount of hurt that you cannot rebuild over. It does not mean everything will be perfect, but it means you deserve to live a healed and thriving life despite what you have been through. If anything, you deserve it more now than ever because of the time that was taken from you when you were a child. Once you have pinpointed where your major issues stem from, you can begin to peel back layer after layer. This takes a different level of courage and vulnerability so if you have made it this far, I am proud of you. The healing process is day to day, but your life will begin to flourish in ways you never thought possible if you stick with the process of holding yourself accountable and making better choices. The universe tremendously rewards people who push past their fears—those who chase their dreams and those who do the uncomfortable things for the betterment of themselves and humanity. You become the best version of you and offer the world the best of yourself. May this be the end of ignorance, the start of healing, and the beginning of true happiness.

CHAPTER 3
Blue Bloods:
The Most Violent Gang
in America

Growing up in New York in the early 2000s, you see early on how to deal with the police, as we were bombarded with images and videos of police brutality and abuse of power. We learned to duck behind cars or cross the street after school to avoid them. Officers were essentially supposed to be first responders, just like ambulance drivers or fire fighters, but we did not grow up with the luxury of viewing them as superheroes; instead we saw them as neighborhood terrorists. For the first 11 years of my life, I lived around the corner from the 75th precinct, the deadliest and most frequently sued precinct in all of NYC. We watched as they profiled minorities because of the way they looked, pinned drugs and false charges on them to meet arrest quotas, antagonized and intimidated its residents, and harassed women they found attractive by pulling them over and coercing them into doing whatever it was they wanted. We watched the news paint them as servers of Christ, but it was drastically different from what I had witnessed. Even with all the chaos and distrust, you would come across a few amazing officers who moved you so much they would make you think differently for a while. As teens, we believed these mean officers were just looking for somebody to release their anger out on, but as an adult I understood there had always been a much bigger devil at play. When you are racist, you have bias and prejudices that do not allow you to see people as people, but only what you were taught about them. This clouds your judgment, compassion, and respect for others who are different from you. These stereotypes may seem insignificant, but they matter deeply. A dangerous white teen is considered a troubled boy who is learning the hard lessons by making mistakes. He is considered quirky and cute for trying new things and getting in trouble while he was young instead of older. These "cute mishaps" can include driving while drunk, robbery, assault, murder, and rape. They believe these boys are just getting it out of their system early, and since they come from two parent homes in the suburbs, they are believed to come from "good" families. A black teen is not allowed room for any mistakes. Not a broken tail light, not speeding or making the wrong turn, not walking with headphones or playing in the park, not being lost or needing directions. Black skin has inherently been seen as a threat so they are never given the same compassion as others. They believe you are a menace and actively looking for trouble so it does not matter what you do to be deemed aggressive, they have already made up their minds about you before you open your mouth. The difference in charges can show you just how sick the system is. A white teen, who rapes a woman, is slapped on the wrist, but a black boy who is walking home is killed for simply looking *suspicious*. Black boys are not given the freedom to live with the naïve thought process of a child's mind because they are viewed and treated as menaces, so while white parents are building lemonade stands, black parents are removing hoodies from their children's wardrobes and teaching them how to navigate in a world that perceives them as scary just for existing. They watch the innocence of their children ripped away right before their eyes, as going biking is no longer a fun ride with your friends, but menacing instead because people will think you are riding around looking for trouble. Trips to buy your favorite toys are no longer fun when you realize you are being followed around the whole time. Their childhood is ripped like a rug from under them, and they are expected to adjust to this cruel way of life and be alright. White women have historically been painted in the image of innocent, docile, and feminine creatures, who are always the damsels in distress in the middle of chaos, although they are often the ones who created it. So many innocent black people have died at the accusations of evil white women. While they have never lifted a finger, they hold tears so powerful it ends in bloodshed. Lies that lead to lynchings… America's Sweetheart. While black women have been historically perceived as angry, promiscuous, masculine, and stupid, they are the most educated demographic in our country and the least protected. This stereotype historically has led to people treating black women like punching bags and dumpsters for the world's issues and problems, even going as far as being viewed as less feminine than women of other races. Many doctors even believe black women have a higher tolerance for pain and over-exaggerate when in emergency rooms. There are extremely damaging stereotypes surrounding black women as angry that have been used as a gas lighting and silencing tactic from the oppressor to make you believe you are unbalanced for wanting their feet off of your neck. In this society as a black woman, you watch the world steal everything from you and then hide their hands to help you look for it. This stereotype makes many young black girls grow up to be women who do not speak up for themselves out of fear of being viewed this way, so they keep their opinions to themselves or try to walk on eggshells so they don't ever project this image of a mad black woman. While black men begin to internalize the way the world treats them, they try to make themselves smaller or invisible. They begin to cross the street before white people do or wait for the next elevator so they won't cause another to feel uncomfortable; they walk ahead of you so you know they aren't following you. Racism is not just in the prison system, but it is a global disease and every part of our lives and jobs are infested with it. No matter what part of the world you land in, there is a bias against dark skin. In India, colorism runs rampant, and lightening creams are sold by the millions. Our views shape our judgment and the way we look at the world, so it matters in the roles we play in society. So you can see how a racist who spends their time drinking and justifying murder from his porch is not as threatening as a judge who can use his position to cause immense pain. Police brutality is just the tip of the iceberg as racist judges are an entire evil force on their own. I got to see firsthand the power dynamics at play in this country. On June 5th of 2020, a few friends and myself planned a protest in honor of Breonna Taylor, a young black woman who was shot in her apartment as she was asleep with her boyfriend. The cops entered her apartment with a no-knock warrant, looking for a drug dealer who was already in custody. Three plain clothes officers ran inside un-announced and fired eight shots into her body. She was left there for seven minutes unattended before she ultimately died. The only person arrested that night was her boyfriend, who had already suffered the tragedy of watching the love of his life die in front of him. We led two starting points for the protest in honor of her life on what would have been her 27th birthday. Our ending point? The big bad wolf: the 75th precinct. We marched in the pouring rain, in the middle of a pandemic with gloves, masks, and hand sanitizer and watched as people came outside of their homes to show support—Abuelas banging pots and pans outside of their windows, drivers honking their horns and showing fists in solidarity. Although we were in the middle of a global health crisis, people in East New York were making their voices heard.

Photographed by Anna Bradley-Smith

When we arrived, we were greeted with 50 officers behind gates, wearing bulletproof vests, armed to the teeth with guns, zip ties, tear gas, batons, and shield gear. As activists poured their hearts out and young kids from the area came to talk about their experience with the police, the cops showed that they cared by smoking cigars from their windows, pointing and laughing at us. It was an absolute slap in the face to the community they serve, but we quickly knew we were not dealing with humans but gang members with no compassion. At this moment, I could not help but think of police officer Micheal Dowd, one of the most notorious, corrupt cops in the NYPD and the 75th precinct's history, who was convicted of racketeering and conspiracy to distribute narcotics, becoming notorious for stealing from drug dealers, indulging in cocaine, warning murderers and drug dealers about upcoming raids, providing them with guns and fake badges to protect themselves, and keeping police eyes off of them while arresting their opposition. In return, Mr. Dowd was given thousands of dollars and bags of cocaine every week. While a lot of the officers in this department were dirty—they filmed an entire documentary about it—Micheal was boastful. In this documentary, they explained how to be considered a loyal officer was to cover their own. That meant theft, murder, or rape: it did not matter. To be a good cop meant to never make complaints to your supervisors. It meant you abuse your power and create a bond with these officers through dirt, and only the illegal things you have done together connect you. The system was designed to imprison and terrorize us; you cannot give people who are racist and emotionally underdeveloped guns and control over neighborhoods they do not live in with people they do not care about. When I was younger, I was naive as to how profitable the prison industry was. A billion dollar booming business, America's backbone. Shortly after slavery was abolished, large prisons were built by the thousands all over the United States, and the prisons they began building needed to be filled. So they started by making laws that turned people in prison into state property. This would force them to work for free and essentially took away most of their basic human rights. They started to arrest black Americans and immigrants by the thousands on minuscule charges; things as simple as looking an officer in the eyes was taken as grounds that you were trying to intimidate—using anything that could stick on record and keep them in the system so parole would plague their lives. It was not about taking bad people off the streets but filling the empty beds in jail so they did not lose any money. White slave owners did not know what to do with themselves after they lost what they deemed was their "property." Although they were paid $300 for every slave who was freed, which in 2019 is equivalent to $8,000 per person, this was not enough for them. This resulted in millions of dollars in reparations for white slave owners and none for the black people forced to create, build, and maintain this country at the cost of their lives, bodies, and children. It is asinine to believe that the descendants of the people who forcefully built this country should not be given what they were owed, but the great-great-grandsons and daughters of slave owners are still benefiting from the payouts today. This country has not hidden its hate nor have they apologized for it. While millions of black people were tortured, denied the rights to read, write, or learn, many found ways to do it in secret. When they were stripped from their culture and taught to believe everything about them was inherently evil and ugly, they fought to keep traditions and instead celebrated their culture in private until they had the freedom to do so publically. It took a long time to realize and accept that the foundation of America never had an interest in building up a society but instead profited from our pain and misery. The system is not broken; it is working the way it was intended to.

Most minorities become cops because of what they experienced as kids or young adults. They wanted to

change the racist system in impoverished neighborhoods and thought becoming a part of it would help
heal the community. They were not wrong. Good cops
do their best to understand and especially respect the
people they are looking after. A good cop builds a
bridge of trust and respect between the community and
the department. A good cop chooses his morals and
conscience over a paycheck. Good cops do not remain
silent in the name of blue but stand by their character. A good cop leaves in the name of honor. Good
cops understand the abuse we face because they see
it for themselves. They do not put on a blue uniform
and suddenly lose all sense of reality or accountability.
Good cops know a call to defund police departments
is smart because they believe in the advancement of
our communities. They understand it does not mean
the end of protection for our neighborhoods or leaving
criminals out on the street, but rather it means to redis-
tribute a large portion of the hundreds of billions of
dollars taxpayers spent on cool new gun gear and move
it into places that can help our communities thrive. To
take a percentage of these billions and use it to help
the homeless, addicts, and people with mental health
issues find stability. This would also mean we would
need less police activity patrolling and harassing our
communities as these people will be getting the help
they need and would not be out on the streets. It means
moving these funds towards people who need help
long enough for them to get back on their feet and putting money back into our schools so our kids have the
necessary tools they need in order to grow and learn.

Investing in after school programs will keep them busy and teach them life skills and important lessons. It means to pay teachers an actual living wage, so they are not pulling scraps from their paychecks to get things for children who are not theirs, and to create a healthy place our children could thrive in. It means to build a society we do not need to heal from. I cannot for the life of me understand why our Government would rather see more chaos and death than they would like to see the advancement and healing of their citizens. It is *almost* as if there are trillions of dollars made from the pain, misery and poverty of its people. Which great America were they so eager to get back? The America that profited from our pain, or the America that began killing us when we told them to stop?

CHAPTER 4
Saving the Children:
The Protection of Pedophiles

There is a sinister game at play that profits and enjoys the global suffering and abuse of children. Illegal child labor laws, sex trafficking, pedophilia, mental, physical, and so many other forms of abuse. In the Caribbean, the exploitation of these children starts when they learn to walk as millions of tourist fly in each year in the hope of fulfilling their long lived, sick fantasies; things that would usually have them burned alive back home are somehow not morally wrong if the children cannot speak the same language. Pedophiles understand the naive minds of children and exactly how to get what they want, so they hold money, material items, and power over children and women who have lived in poor countries all of their lives. They target vulnerable kids who are just looking to work for themselves and their families. Most of these children have been on there own and feeding themselves since they could walk by selling small goods. For children who are misplaced, homeless, dealing with mental health issues, or have suffered rape, abuse, or other life altering experiences, someone coming in to swoop and "save" them seems like the glory. Their pain is used against them because pedophiles know children do not understand manipulation and believe everyone is pure. These people think that soliciting minors for sex is not as vile if it is not done to children deemed innocent; since these children are on the street, they believe the excuses they make for themselves. They fly in by the millions each year with their privilege, arrogance—and more than anything—the fucking audacity. They try to trap poor young teens and adults into this incredible lie of the American Dream and the riches they come with from all around the world.

Unfortunately, there are many racist dynamics at play that allow these men and women to come into the Caribbean and take advantage of our children. They treat our young girls and boys as meals to satisfy their hunger and return back home just in time for Sunday service. Do not get me wrong: children from all over the world have been under-protected and violated by adults, and there are no moral ground rules for pedophilia, but there is an extreme bias and carelessness when the victims are black and brown children. Old white men fly into these islands with the intent of taking advantage of the girls and women, while white women fly in by the millions to fulfill their sick sexual fantasies with black men. These are usually the same racist white women who clutch their purses as they walk by in New York but now have become infatuated with the danger of having sex with them. These racist women will still want you dead or thrown in jail when they get back home, but if these men could give them a mixed race baby to parade around as her "I am not racist" card before they go, it would be amazing. Not only are they pedophiles, but they are racist too.

In the Dominican Republic, there are layers depending on what you are looking for, so old pedophiles come in and make offers for young boys while white women play a huge part in sexual violence towards black and native men. Young girls are almost immediately tossed into this life of exchanging sex for survival, and grown women who were coerced and violated as young girls now make their living doing the same. It is so normalized that many hotel workers participate in the trafficking of these children. These "hotel clerks" are paid and told by the tourists what they are looking for and how much they are willing to spend. It is their job to go out and find it. I remember visiting the island as a young girl and watching my older cousins parade my young brothers around older women, insisting that they take their pick. It did not matter that they were children; the fact is they were boys, and this is what the women wanted, right? These car rides consisted of showcasing the variety of women they could choose from each hour, yelling at random girls as we drove by and introducing women to boys in hopes they would reward them with sex. There is this incredibly cruel and normalized thought process that we put our young boys through. Too many stories have come out about men taking their sons, nephews, or cousins on a field trip to lose their virginity with grown women, supposedly as a bonding tool between the men in the family. Since society has taught us that men are sex-crazed animals who have instincts they cannot control, it is simply glanced over. They fail to see these kids as just that—children whose brains and bodies are still developing. These kids' minds have no idea as to what sex is, and they have not even begun to learn about themselves or how to navigate this world, so how would they know what consent is or the importance of self-control? Society simply teaches them that the act of sex itself is what makes them a man. These women, who are usually in their 20s and 30s, have sex with boys as young as 11 or 12. These women are adults who were most likely groomed this way as children themselves and have now continued the damaging cycle. For many boys it can change their perception of life, manhood, sex, and women forever. These young boys might go on to become men who lead lives of self-destruction themselves and also damage the people they come in contact with as they grow up with many issues stemming from being sexually abused: anxiety, depression, lack of self-control, deeply rooted intimacy issues, and becoming sexually or physically violent.

This is not just in the Dominican Republic or in the Caribbean but all over the world. Lil Wayne spoke about being a child and having grown women perform sexual acts on him because his father figure (and manager at the time) sent them in. Boosie stated he got an older woman to perform sexual acts on his 12-year-old son because it was done to him as a child and he believed this would "save" him from being gay. He believed this was the right way, so the vicious cycle just continues. There are countless other stories just like this.

As traumatizing as these things are when you are a child, boys are not given the space to speak up about this kind of abuse as they get older. For most of these men, when speaking up about sexual assault, rape, or physical and verbal abuse, they are met with laughter and ridicule. Their pain is taken lightly since boys are told that sex is their primary nature. Because women can be viewed as delicate flowers who cannot perpetuate or even have the strength to be abusive, these stories are brushed off or even given high fives and congratulations if the woman who assaulted them was pretty enough. For boys who are molested and assaulted by other men, the shame can run extremely deep and cause a lot of confusion, homophobia, distrust, and hatred for men.

On the other side of this sickness are girls as young as 11, who have been groomed since toddlers to believe the only way to elevate in society is to use their bodies and sexuality to survive. These old men use the girls' poor living conditions and lack of resources to get what they want and take advantage, knowing these young girls left abusive families and toxic homes to fend for themselves. It has become a trend and a sick joke to list Dominican women as the things you are going to buy on your tickets when flying into the island, and it makes me incredibly angry to see the misfortune and exploitation of our homeland somehow become a running joke instead of a source of outrage. Many Dominican Americans do this too as they travel in craving power just like *they* taught us. They walk around with a certain arrogance because they hold money over the heads of women suffering through poverty. It is an incredibly twisted game at the expense of others. Adults blame and shame young girls, who are overly sexualized, abused, or raped, for the things that happen to them. So many girls are victims of abuse and have not been met with the compassion needed to heal; instead, their families have thrown them to the wolves. Instead of addressing, healing, and holding adults accountable. Society calls these children every word related to whore in the book. Older women can be notorious for being extremely cruel to young girls, just as people once were to them. They believe that these girls are asking for it and not that they are still kids, who may be promiscuous because of past abuse and other traumas. Young girls are usually left to defend themselves on the streets and are not given the proper kind of compassion, guidance, or tools to heal themselves but instead are met with disgust, blame, and anger. You cannot hold children accountable for the actions of grown men and women.

If something like this happens to you, you can become one of two different kinds of people. While some felt this pain and never wanted to feel it again, they chose to end it within themselves and heal; others have chosen to repeat the cycle of abuse and continue to hurt others. I am disappointed in the adults who failed them, as most of these children are kids who left home because of abuse or neglect. When there are children who have no idea what the results of having sex are, and grown men are constantly preying on them, many things like STDs and pregnancies occur. This is how most of these kids end up on the street, trying to provide for themselves and their children. There are some people who spend thousands of dollars strictly to have sex with teenagers in countries where they can get away with it due to poor criminal justice systems. I would just like to say that if you have to travel thousands of miles away to sleep with anybody who will give you the chance, you do not need to have sex—you need sage, 9,000 bee stings to the heart, and a lemon juice eye mask! It pains me, but I realize that this is a system in which women have learned to adapt because of the circumstances they were forced into after being denied their rights to work, learn, and lead. Slut shaming in the Dominican Republic is our second language. Every girl or woman you come across is *un maldito cuero*. It is normal to victim-blame girls because of their circumstances, but one thing is for sure: I will not hold young children accountable for the actions of grown men and women. When you have a fully developed and functioning brain, you know exactly how manipulation and coercion work, how a child's mind respects and listens to adults—and you use this to your advantage. In New York it was normal to watch your 15-year-old friends get picked up from school by their 25-year-old "boyfriends." If you are a teenager and you are reading this and have dealt with older men trying to wheel you in, I beg you to run. You can ask any grown women why older men date young girls, and they will always tell you: it is because these men can be extremely underdeveloped or abusive, so a woman who has been through situations and learned through trial and error can pick up on red flags and see the signs, but a young girl has no knowledge of vindictiveness and cannot tell them apart. Men cannot control a woman who has her own set of values, morals, and standards, so they want to train and mold you from a girl into what they believe is a woman. We need to reinvest in the protection and healing of our communities and young children. We need to get rid of the corrupt and weak criminal justice system that allows it, the people who normalize and turn a blind eye to it, and the people who take advantage of it. We can begin by giving young girls and boys better opportunities if they are out on the streets and fending for themselves. We can teach them to heal from the inaction of the adults around them and show them how to highlight their skills and passions while working on themselves. We can do our best to teach our children about sexual education and consent. Our job as adults is to protect the seeds that come after us. So first, we can begin by following the footsteps of the Dominican police department that followed Theodore Symonds back into the states after his friend from the Dominican Republic found him preying on young girls. They sentenced him to 17 years for the assault of 13- and 15-year-old girls. It is only one of many cases of abuse, but we can start by following these pedophiles back home, arresting and charging them for their actions—and then banning them from ever being able to come back to the Dominican Republic, or places like it. The normalization of pedophilia has lasted long enough, and way too many children have been scarred by it. From the creep at family reunions to the CEOs and the sexual predators in churches, you will no longer be allowed to live in silence.

Morir Soñando:

I crave your cold beer and warm sun,
How cafe con pan is a 6 star breakfast,
But does not taste the same if not served by an elder.
How your mornings start at 5, but here time is slowed
    down.
You feel at peace and calm, not tired or sleepy.
Is it Mama? Switching an anxiety powered alarm clock
To *Abuela*'s sweet voice, may be the change I need.
I pull up a seat as she tells me her dream from
    the night before,
She has always been an amazing storyteller.
She talks with an ancient kind of peace, so I am hanging
    on to every word,
There is a certain calmness in the air,
As if the rest of the world has not woken up yet.
Lla, la gallina se levanto and the *paleta* man is making
    his first round.
As someone who is used to being woken up
    by police sirens,
This is music to my ears.
I was born in the "United" States,
Where they constantly tell people like us,
To go back to where we came from.
As a first generation American Dominican,
Our train commutes to work are full of daydreaming,
Being on a rocking chair back on the warm island,
    con una fria.
Your *Tios* and *Tias* giving you seven years worth of love
    in two weeks,
Makes you want to never come back.
It is funny, how my parents left you for the betterment
    of our lives,

And now we spend our life
Racing back to you every chance we get.
When I was five, I got on a plane and visited what
        I thought was a foreign place.
In all of my years growing up, I had never seen
        my parents so excited.
I stepped off the plane with Mami and Papi
One on each side, leading me by my small hands.
I felt an immediate rush of hot air hit my face.
I am greeted by warm and joyful faces I had never
        seen before,
A woman pinches my cheeks.
"Oh Mai Gaaa! Igualita! Que bella! Di Sion Tia!" she says.
I do not recognize her, but her voice feels familiar.
Everyone has spent my life telling me,
I look just like my father.
For the first time ever,
I look around at twenty faces that look just like me,
I realize at this exact moment—
I am home.

Illustration by Jamcy Stephen Maquilon

CHAPTER 5
Mending An Island:
Healing the Dominican Republic

The Dominican Republic is one of the most beautiful places on this earth. It is full of crystal clear beaches, the most amazing food, and most importantly, the greatest people you will ever meet. Our elders walk the island handing out wisdom like *paletas;* the river is God's personalized gift to us. The island is full of beauty, color, and corruption. I went to school in East New York. In P.S. 345, there was a melting pot of cultures, languages, and people where we had never thought about our differences because we were surrounded by it. This school included immigrant children from around the world; because we were all different shades, spoke different languages, and brought foods of different cultures to lunch, it was not out of the ordinary although every now and then we took jabs at each other with stereotypical jokes. We never believed one was better than the other, just different. In my culture we never spoke about race; I was simply Dominican. I never questioned anything outside of it because I was taught we danced Bachata, mixed orange juice with milk for breakfast, and spoke Spanish. I remember being in middle school and hearing my black American friends tell me Dominicans were just Jamaicans who spoke Spanish. It was funny to me then, but it was not until I grew up that I started to ask my own questions and do my own research about why there was such hostility and racism against dark skin in our culture. I learned quickly that it had been intentionally hidden from us, and that the history of Tainos and Africans living in our island was information that had been removed from our history books; because of it, our island and its people still suffer. The moment you walk down a block in the Dominican Republic, you see a variety of different shades and can't help but wonder, where are we really from? Growing up I realized that my family events looked like a block party, a clash of cultures. I have an uncle who looks like the poorest version of Denzel Washington and a cousin so white he looks like he came from Cracker Barrel's management team. Taino Indians, who were later enslaved when Spaniards invaded our island, originally inhabited the Dominican Republic. They were on the brink of extinction because they were dying due to being mistreated, raped, dehydrated, starved, and riddled with diseases due to being kept in inhumane conditions by the Spaniards. This is when the Spaniard Conquistadores later forcefully brought in close to 12.5 million Africans into North America, the Caribbean, and South America. The Spaniards went on to rape and procreate with both Taino and African women, creating what are the descendants of this mix of people who dwell on our island today. While anti-blackness is global, things got really bad on our island when our most cruel dictator, Trujillo, came into office: he is one of the longest lasting scars of our country. He was a man who had his pictures photo shopped to make him look whiter and hated anything related to blackness. His main methods of control included no free speech, no opposition, and no free press. Anyone who challenged or opposed him was killed and so were their families. He launched an anti-black campaign that targeted Haitians and dark-skinned Dominicans to "cleanse" the island of them and their history. He put in policies that classified Dominicans as white and started an immigration program to bring in thousands of white women to live and procreate on the island so he could "rid" the culture of our African history—which will never happen. It is 2020, and it is more present in our music, art, food, and culture than it has ever been. The Dominicans who did try to identify as black in their documents were met with backlash from officials. Dr. Dickhead's war on blackness began with listing news articles and posters that painted Haitians to be violent, dirty rapists who were here to steal and take over the island. Trujillo believed they were sub-human and animal-like. He brainwashed people into believing they were not deserving of love, respect, health, or compassion due to the way they lived and the culture they practiced. His propaganda went on for years to destroy the minds of millions—so much so that his theories and ideologies are still believed and practiced until this day. He began the poisoning of his people's minds so they would become desensitized to the thousands of people he would later go on to kill. In October of 1937, he ordered his army to go out and slaughter every Haitian they saw, and it did not matter whether you were a man, woman, or child. His determining factor as to whether you would live or die was if you could pronounce the word *perejil*—which means parsley in Spanish. The only difference is that Dominicans were conquered by Spain, so we speak Spanish, and the French conquered Haitians, so they speak Creole. Dominicans pronounce it "Pe-r-ejil" and Haitians pronounced it Pe-l-ejil". The *R* and the *L* difference determined whether you were killed or not. This massacre went on to be called "the Cutting" because not one bullet was used, and the soldiers only used machetes. It is still until this day one of the vilest and most disgusting atrocities that is hidden from our history and not spoken about on our island. A lot of Dominicans in that time did not know what was happening as the local news were never allowed to broadcast the slaughters due to being under tyranny. We have been taught a whitewashed history and stuffed with hateful propaganda towards our own so much that Dominicans have suppressed a lot of their heritage and culture due to brainwashing, assimilation, and fear. Did you think Dominican women being the blowout kink-removing Queens was a coincidence? I was raised around women who thought that someone seeing their natural hair was a sin. As if there curls were a curse. Lightening creams are a top seller and running from the sun is an

Olympic sport so they don't get any darker. They will go to great lengths to remove any trace of blackness and are still very much fighting this war with themselves today. We have suppressed the beauty and survival of our black and Indian ancestors while upholding the white supremacist values of those who enslaved and then erased our history. It is asinine to keep these conversations private in our living rooms. Although there is a new awakening happening and we are progressing slowly, we must first learn our history, be honest with ourselves and how we have dealt with discrimination in our own lives, and how we have done it to others as well. This means to do the internal work of unlearning your prejudices and removing preconceived notions about blackness for what they truly are. This will take a lot of inside work to dismantle, but you can soon remove values that were never truly yours to begin with. In the Dominican Republic, hair is everything. I spent my entire childhood being yanked from the scalp and did not see my natural hair in its chemical free state until I turned 21. The smell of a relaxer still haunts my spirit, and I smell it in my nightmares. These images of straight hair and light skin being the standard for beauty is still very much present. The darker you are, the more your hair kinks up, and the worse you are treated. These stereotypes have poisoned our minds and infiltrated every part of our lives, from school, to work, to church—even the networks and programs that are supposed to be for the advancement of us do a huge disservice by highlighting white supremacist values. They play into the ignorance of our people and ancient stereotypes. Growing up around Dominicans meant randomly hearing *"De Lo Mio Primo! Como Estas?"* outside and then realizing these people did not even know each other. This is just how we greeted each other; you being one of us made us instantly brothers or sisters. *"Sientate! Agarra un plato que llegaste a buen tiempo!"* Grab a seat and a plate." It is probably the thing I love most about my people. We are instantly connected and at home with each other. We never let one go without food, *una tacita de café*, or a shot of *mamajuana*. So I did not understand how some could treat each other this way and then see another black person and be prejudice. They were the same people after all, living in the same neighborhood, both immigrants, same skin complexions, and similar struggles of moving to a different country to fulfill a dream for them and their family. The only difference is that one was from Trinidad and the other was from the Dominican Republic. I could not understand... our only boundary being language. It showed me how much disconnect existed among us even though we fight most of the same struggles.

I am finishing this book in the middle of a national outburst of protest in honor of George Floyd, who was killed by police. As he begged to breathe and yelled out for his deceased mother, the nation went up in flames. Millions of people from all around the world came out to protest for him and all the black people who have been killed at the hands of the police. In a turn of events, a small group of Dominicans in New York formed a community circle with neighborhood "leaders" to stand by at night and call out any suspicious activity regarding looters and thieves. They wanted to protect their neighborhood and the stores that were owned by minorities, who were mostly immigrants. It was awesome to see the community come together in the form of protection.... at first. The next day, a mob of 30 people armed to the teeth with bats chased out three black teens because they did not recognize them. They assumed they were stealing because they were black and outside; we had to remind them that this is not the 1930s and they are not Trujillo's army. Racism coming from Latinos always seemed to amaze me as we know that officers will not ask you if you speak Spanish before they shoot you. Growing up I did not understand the internalized hatred as the proudest parts of our culture came from the enslaved Africans on our islands who fought so hard to keep these traditions. The food, music, spirituality and people they tried to teach us to hate so much, looked just like us because they were *us*. The brainwashing that racist adults teach you is subtle at first, something as small as denying you access to Black culture or going as far as associating Hip Hop and anything else created by black people with violence and stupidity. It starts with kids bringing home their black friends and having their parents treat them badly or not allowing them to come back. When you begin dating as a teenager, you can start to hear things like "Tienes que avanzar la raza" as advice. A vile saying Trujillo coined and far too many have internalized and dragged with them throughout the years. To "advance our race" means to date as white as possible to make lighter children with no signs of black features. They believe the closer in proximity you are to whiteness, the more beautiful and successful you can be. It starts with treating young black Latinas kinks and curls as something that needs to be covered or altered at all times and brown kids being treated differently than their lighter skinned cousins. This is how you raise a racist who will think profiling black people somehow makes them a superhero. We have come to an awakening and shift of silence where young Dominicans living all over the world have begun denouncing racist ideoligies, proudly claiming their blackness, while sharing their honest experiences and holding political figures and family accountable. Black Americans are with us on the front lines of our Anti-ICE protests and many of the other issues that affect our communities. They fight alongside us because they understand what it feels like to be in mourning and pain and to not be able to get justice after life. These are not the Oppression Olympics; we do not need to compare them but realize instead how similar our struggles are. We are all fighting for the same thing—freedom. The following week, thousands of Dominicans stepped up to denounce this kind of behavior; they began a protest in Dyckman the following week in solidarity with Black Lives Matter where Dominicans and Haitians led the way with their flags tied together, showcasing a new generation of unity. It was one of the most beautiful things I had ever witnessed, and I have seen Beyoncé live. For some black Americans who do not know the history of the Caribbean, they can deny and treat black

Latinos as outsiders trying to get in or not accepting them as brothers and sisters because of the language barrier and past experiences with racist Latinos. For us all to begin truly moving forward we must unlearn the mess we have been taught and reteach ourselves. Pick up books, watch videos, ask questions, and then bring these conversations to the living rooms where our people are usually the most embolden and comfortable. It is up to you to reach those closest to you and hold them accountable because I can't reach them and neither will a politician in a suit. It has to come from you, a familiar face, a voice they know and love. It starts with us and while we do not have to be delicate with our elders, we must have patience. Make teaching and speaking to children your priority. It will take a lot longer to teach and reach our old heads than it will our young ones, and while we have a long road ahead of us, somebody has got to do it. Surprise... it's you, bitch!

CHAPTER 6
The Privilege of Choice:
Eso no es de Hombre

eing born a woman means to be bombarded with rules and regulations to abide by before you even understand what being a girl is. When you are young, they make it seem like if you do not follow the rules put in place for you, everything will be downhill from there on. It is not for you to understand, as there are certain guidelines that were made a long time ago to ensure you stayed in your place and never questioned anything outside of it. You must look, talk, act, and dress a certain way to be considered a "real" woman. It is one of the things you never understand as a child, but just become used to as time passes. I remember being young and having to do house work while my brothers went out to play. I remember finally mustering up enough courage to ask my dad why they could not do the chores this one time. Here it was: the first time I had heard it. *"Eso no es de hombre,"* he said. "That is not for men." *Que diablo se significa eso?* What the hell does that mean? As if kitchens had dick repellents that shot at them every time they tried to step inside. Even as a child I had always asked myself why my girl cousins had to stay upstairs and could not go outside to play but instead had to cook, clean, and look after children younger than they were as if they were third parents. Something about a three-year-old cooking for an infant did not sit right in my spirit.

Now while these are all things you need to learn how to do to survive in the world when you become older, society has tricked us into believing this is a woman's job and comes natural, so we have begun molding little girls into future mothers, instead of women. Many women who were raised like this can become ultimate "yes" women. They feel responsible for everybody around them and put others before themselves. They over-extend themselves even when they also need help. They treat everybody like their own child, who they need to protect. This is bad for many reasons, as people with negative intentions can latch on to you and run you dry. Side note: There should never be gender-enforced chores because we need all of these to navigate through life and to survive. Just as you do not want your daughter to grow up to become her husband's maid, who secretly hates him for being a lazy bitch, you also do not want your son to be secretly hated by his wife for being a lazy bitch. This is how your coffee ends up with rat poison instead of sugar. We should give children, when of age, equal responsibility so they learn how to survive and not how to do these things solely to take care of someone else. These girls usually become women who never had the time to figure out what they liked, disliked, or wanted to do with their lives because their life was full of chaos, and then it became normal. So they keep looking for people to fix, heal, and take care of. If you walk down the girls' aisle in a toy store, you will find hundreds of kitchen sets, Easy Bake ovens, baby dolls with Pampers, fake milk, and carriages. We are not true to this; we're groomed to this. When we become teenagers, we are told what to wear and what we deserve based on it. If it is 100 degrees out and you have on shorts, to our elders you're a whore *sin verguenza*—a woman who is begging to be harassed. This kind of language is nothing new to our ears as we are used to hearing *"Ve cambiate que hay hombre en la casa"* since as far back as we can remember. *"Go get dressed, men are here."* I always wondered, what kind of men do you have in your house? This tone has become so normal that we spend more time policing what young girls wear and not discussing why you allow a pedophile to sit comfortably in your home. They tell us to tone it down because women are prettier when they are quiet. They tell you not to explore or play outside because you will mess up your hair and then the boys won't like you. They tell you to take up as little space as possible—physically and mentally. This means to not question anything outside of what you are told to do because a woman who talks back is a woman nobody wants. The list of rules gets longer and more ridiculous as you grow older. You know how bad it has gotten when brainwashed women enforce these same roles and consider you less because of it.

I remember being at family events where I was bombarded by some of the older women in my family on how to act and dress to attract what I needed to settle down and, finally, be happy. They told me my main priority should be to find a good man, buy a house, and pop out a few sex souvenirs to take care of and look after. (A "good man" is coded language to these women. He can be abusive, have children outside of his marriage, and treat you terribly, but if he provides for your home financially, he is a God-sent man in their eyes.) They told me to look after my home, feed my husband, raise the kids, and then I will have graduated into womanhood. These are the things they believed made you whole—that a woman by herself is just a woman waiting for her husband. It is engraved in our minds to believe that marriage and romantic relationships are our final purpose. These women did not care about the things I loved or dreamed about: the cakes I made to celebrate them, the books I wanted to write to save their daughters, the truth I spoke to power on behalf of them. They never asked me about any accomplishments or goals I had in my heart; they just asked me *"Y el novio?"* three times a week. They assured me that they never had to worry about a car note or rent, and this is why they were happy. I knew then the price they paid was much bigger. The dreams, passions, and ideas that haunted them at night... Their respect and dignity was the tax they had paid for staying with a man who disrespected and mistreated them, all for the sake of keeping the lights on. I saw what this had created in my family, which was incredible women with contagious spirits, angel-like energy and amazing ideas that they put to bed early to take care of the people in their lives. Growing up I loved and despised these women at the same time. I saw what they brought and how they were treated for it. They were gorgeous, intelligent, funny, and charismatic. The selflessness they showed was both admirable and scary. It was beautiful because they were compassionate and helped others when they needed it the most; this is where I had learned it. They were God-fearing women who served their church before anything, so it was scary to see people constantly take from them and never look behind to see if they needed it back. It made me resent them for not standing up for themselves. I could not understand for the life of me why they would allow others to treat them this way.

When I got older, the more I learned about these women and our history, I realized the privilege of choice was what most of them did not have. They had been groomed from childhood and sent into arranged marriages at early ages, never having the freedom I now have today to say no. Back in the Dominican Republic, post-Trujillo era (and still, today), women who rebelled against any form of authority were killed. To say no to your father, brother, or husband made you liable to be killed by them or the government. To not follow tradition or do as you were told was to tarnish your family name. I understand why they are the way they are, and why I turned out the way I am. I had the pleasure of having other aunts who would stroll into these same family events late, fine, half drunk, and laughing like the world was their playground. As if nobody had spent years stealing their joy. They were the ones who pulled me aside after the others filled my head with a timeline as to why I must have children by 25 and swiftly told me *"Esto hombres no sirven ni para morirse! Has lo que tu quiera." "Girl, these men can't even die correctly. Do whatever you want!"* There was something intriguing about women who did not follow the rules or went against the grain, the ones who did not change their last names, the ones who chose themselves over men who did not bring them joy. The ones who chose themselves over timelines put on them advising when to bring a child into this world. The ones who lost everything because they chose to lead a life they loved over a life that looks good on the outside. This is what I wanted: the freedom to choose. To me, they were the most powerful beings in this oppression-filled world. But by sexist standards, they were whores with no purpose. A woman without a husband and children is supposed to be sad, so if you enjoy your own company, you are mentally unstable. I learned soon enough that there was no correct way to be a woman. That these imaginary rules placed in front of us no longer held the weight they once did. We realize now that women can be complex beings who can be more than one thing. You get to make the decisions over your own life. For a woman whose joy is to be a stay-at-home mom, she gets to take care of her home, husband, and children and be proud of it because this is what makes her happy. You can be a woman who may never want children and has spent most of your time building a legacy for yourself outside of it. This makes you happy because it is your choice. Your main question to yourself should always be "What do you want out of this life?" Not what your parents want from you... Not what your brother or girlfriend wants out of you... Make sure the answer is coming from your heart and is not somebody else's idea for you. You deserve to live an abundant life that you're proud of, and nobody should guilt you into believing you're less of a woman because of your decisions. The beauty of learning and growing out of these shackles is realizing that we no longer have to choose things we do not want. You never had to choose between being intelligent or having a lot of fun, between building a business or having a family. For so long women were made to believe you could only be one or the other. I hope you learn how to choose your life outside of respectability politics.

CHAPTER 7
American Patriotism:
The War Against Honesty

L ike most immigrants my parents came to this country with the American dream in mind. They were
painted this broad picture of what it's like living in
the beautiful land of opportunity, the United States of
America. An honest working job, a thriving marriage, a
bunch of big-headed kids running around, a white picket
fenced yard, and a safe community. My mom and dad
were born and raised in Bonao, the capital of Monseñor
Nouel in the Dominican Republic. They got married in
their early 20s and shortly afterward moved to Brooklyn,
New York in 1986. One by one my entire family began
arriving here. Although many people on the island go
through poverty, racism, assimilation, and sexism, DR
is also full of some of the most beautiful rivers, views,
food, and people. The culture and energy feels resilient.
While places in the Caribbean were home to many of
our parents, they chose to leave because of the issues
they faced there, mostly escaping violence and poverty. I
see people who left all they knew for a foreign place with

a foreign language. I think about how my heart ripped when I moved from Brooklyn to Queens when I was a teenager, and I cannot imagine the pain in leaving to a different country and what you know as home. This bravery should be met with compassion but is instead met with resentment. Many land here and are met with the harsh reality of a land that is not as welcoming as they thought it would be, but still they moved forward despite the challenges so they could provide for their families. Many of our parents from the islands were raised post-dictatorship and had to suffer many atrocities in silence. To speak up meant to challenge power and put your body, legacy, and family on the line. Many immigrants truly believe the racism they endured was the price they paid to live here. They do not understand our fight with justice and wanting true equality because they think this is just a part of life and falls under the list of many things we have to accept because we cannot change.

My view as a first generation American-Dominican was far different than what my parents were seeing. They thought the police were our superheroes, while I saw them framing my friends. They saw the United States as the land of liberty, but I knew we had the highest number of incarcerated people in the world. They saw a country where they could freely practice their religion, while I watched our Muslim brothers and sisters be beaten and killed. They believed this country fought for its freedom and honored its soldiers, while I watched them kill citizens in other countries and leave our veterans displaced in the streets to deal with their own mental health issues. The United States has caused some of the most horrific tragedies in this world and has tried to throw dirt on the wounds instead of healing them. Now the whole bitch is on fire. A country sitting on the stolen land of Native Americans, built by the hands of enslaved Africans, and held together by the Latin immigrants they hate so much. They tell the descendants of the people who built this country to pull themselves up by their bootstraps, failing to mention they stole the fucking boots too. These were just *some* of the founding crimes of the United States of America, and many of these acts against its citizens have gone unpunished, never even acknowledged by the U.S. government. It is why terror is so normalized here. Between 2015 and 2020, 5,000 people were murdered at the hands of the police. After these lives were stolen, they were then targeted and demonized after death. Old mug shots, parking tickets from 1997, and a schoolyard fight you had when you were 12 are plastered all over news outlets to convince the public why you deserved to be killed. They take our lives and then spend the following months telling the public why you somehow deserved it. They doused us in respectability politics and tried to make us believe that if somehow we all talked, looked, or dressed differently, this would not happen. But they have shown us this is a lie, time and time again. Whether you are one of the most prestigious doctors walking or a homeless man suffering with mental health issues, you deserve to live and not be murdered at the hands of police. America has a nasty way of making you feel like you should if you do not follow the guidelines as far as what they deem respectable. This is just one of the many ways they have glossed over history and made things worse.

Can you imagine going to the hospital for a regular follow-up and realizing you had been sterilized without your consent? This was reality for 1/3 of all the Puerto Rican women who inhabited the island from the 1930s until the 1970s. They simply woke up and were told they would never be able to have children again. This system was developed in order to get rid of qualities the Government and society believed to be undesirable, and people they thought were "extreme breeders." They began by forging signatures, threatening them with deportation, and using evil tactics like making them sign consent forms once out of surgery and dozing from medication. They would also explain the procedures in English and deny them translators to further their confusion. These patients were never allowed to have children; they were never compensated; and they never received justice. While the U.S. paints minorities to be violent, straight, white, Christian men have treated this world like a playground and peoples lives like toys. They have been treated with kid gloves, coddled and protected, all while being histor- ically the most violent species this side of the universe has ever seen. I do not know of a better way to showcase the hate seeping from American soil than Zimmerman after killing a young, black teenager being let off free, sell- ing the gun for a quarter of a million dollars to a short dick bandit, and then going on to become famous in the world of white supremacists by signing Arizona bottles and Skittle packets—exactly what Trayvon Martin had in his pockets when he was murdered. We can easily see what side of history the U.S. has been on as we watch them dismantle the Black Panthers and send its members to jail while protecting and shielding the KKK. On the morning after 45's election, there was a feeling in the air, a sadness you could smell. The world simply felt heavy. Now we are in 2020, four years into this circus, and there are Nazis lynching black people, young children locked in cages, minorities being assaulted and killed by racists, millions of missing children trafficked into pedophile rings, and we are closing in on the deaths of almost 200,000 Americans due to the negligence of his handling of Covid-19. All while Mr. Pulp golfs and talks in circles. We are in the middle of a global health crisis, and we have not been allowed to adjust or grieve properly for our loved ones. As they try to rush children back into the world as test dummies, their parents are scrambling to feed them since they have been out of work for months, with their mental health deteriorating, losing their loved ones, and not being able to honor them properly, or having access to the small things that bring you joy. While sometimes Americans are pictured as insufferable, stupid, lazy, and selfish—and some of this could be true (refer to elected official #45), we are also victims of a vicious capitalist society that puts its profits over its citizens. Americans are suffering and dying because of ego and lack of care for its citizens by the Government. We know that America was never great because there is no point in history where this government has done right by its people. The people in this country are what keep us together: men who patrol our neighborhoods to make sure everybody is safe and also keep tabs on abusive officers; neighbors who do not have much but bring together what they can to feed people who are hungry; people who are living paycheck to paycheck making care packages for the homeless. Our communities are full of leaders who make it their duty to help those in need. We feed each other. We clothe each other. We pray over each other. We protect each other. This is the real America, we are what makes it great.

Bendiciones:

I toss my book bag onto the floor,
Fourth grade is hard but at least finally, I'm home.
"Lee me eso muchachita,"
Papa says as he hands me a letter.
I grab it slowly, in hopes I understand what it says.
Papa watches my body language eagerly,
As my 10-year-old eyes gloss over the words.
The nervousness in his eyes tell a story,
He is waiting for something I don't understand yet.
Being raised by Immigrants is an honor.
I learned early on,
That where others saw broken English,
I saw someone studying two languages.
That the janitors and bus boys who picked up after them,
Used to be teachers and politicians back home.
How the women who sold flowers and icees on the corner,
Were church leaders back home.
How we painted people as stupid,
For not living up to an American standard,
Although they were geniuses in their native tongues.
In my everyday adult life,
I run into people just like papa and mama.
Elders asking to be helped through their eyes..
The smell of nervousness is strong,
It is the same scent I smelled on papa.
I smile and watch their guard drop as they say:
'Mi hija, me puedes ayudar?'
– Claro que si.
I treat them with compassion –
The kind I wish was shown to my mother.
See, when I look at my parents,
I see courage in physical form.

To understand is a privilege.
To help is an honor.
To be a child of immigrants,
Is to be a translator of documents,
Bearer of good or bad news,
And the bridge that connects us all.

Illustration by Jamcy Stephen Maquilon

CHAPTER 8
Bonding over Sexism:
Silence is Insidious

I have lived a long enough life as a woman of color who talks back to encounter my fair share of sexist men. I have met enough of them to know it isn't the guy in the alley with a hoodie that I thought I was supposed to be scared of, but rather people who were in my living rooms, churches, and schools. They looked like my uncles, pastors, and friends. Now we can understand patriarchy being a system meant to keep women subdued and powerless, while still acknowledging how far we have progressed. Although we move throughout this life differently, we all still play a part in keeping this system going strong. There are different levels of sexists, who all work towards the same system, but the most dangerous one is a "hostile sexist." These are guys who hate, degrade, abuse, and eventually kill women. They believe being born male makes them superior beings; they feel as if they deserve to rule the world simply because they were born this way. Penises do not give you superpowers—ask your ex. These men believe they are smarter and more capable of navigating this world because they do not operate by "emotions." These are also some of the angriest people walking this earth, so I would just like to take this moment to remind you that anger is an emotion. Their hate for women fuels their ego, and their dick loses an inch any time a woman tells them no. These kind of guys believe women are unintelligent, dramatic, overly emotional beings who exist to have sex and bare children. Their ego is their crutch, and women are here strictly for their consumption; these kinds of sexist men have been taught their whole lives that they are superior with no external work or achievements to show for it. So they depend on things like financial status, material items, ego boosts, or the women they are sleeping with to define them. They are not hard to spot, as they are usually verbally aggressive and physically violent with women. They use their strength to intimidate but take a much calmer approach to other men—you know why.

Our second contestant in the misogynistic assholes contest is Benevolent Sexists. These come in the form of chivalrous and polite men - with the exception of you staying in your lane as a woman. Do not get this confused, as their respect is conditional and reserved for a specific set of women who follow the rules. It is only given to an extent and depends on how you move through this world. Chivalry can be extremely performative because they are expecting something in return. However, do not get these sexists confused with polite men who are well mannered. Polite men are respectful and civil with everyone they come across because it is ingrained in their character. Nice people are nice people no matter who is in front of them or what they can offer. You will be able to tell the difference between the two if you just step back and watch how they treat the people who have nothing to offer them. This "respect" for women is conditioned on whether or not they are attracted to you, related to them, or how close in proximity you are to another man in his life whom he actually loves and respects. This is why I never understood the self-proclaimed nice guys because "hey beautiful" becomes "stupid bitch" shortly afterward. This love for women is wrapped up in respectability politics and covered in shit. If you cannot give a basic level of respect to women without expecting something in return, you are not a nice person: you are a clown without a costume. It is funny to grow up around a family of men who spoke about other women like dogs but would treat the us like royalty. Even as a child I thought it was hypocritical as those women were somebody's nieces and daughters just like we are. So the only thing that protected me from their wrath was my last name. Sorry, *pendejaso*, but you do not get to damage and disrespect every woman you come across and then be offended when it happens to one you love. After all, this is a culture you have kept alive.

These are usually the same fellas who "believe in equality," but think women are incapable of leadership positions as we do not have the capacity to make decisions without letting emotions hinder us. There are some men who want equality but do not care about it enough to change destructive behaviors or hold their brothers and friends accountable. I'm talking about the men who feel uneasy with the vile remarks or things done by their friends or family, just not enough to tell them why it wasn't okay. So you turn the cheek or try to laugh the awkwardness off. The problem with not calling attention to problematic things is there is a crowd laughing instead of leaving, so it rids them of any guilt because everyone else thinks it is okay. Now these types of fellas are not our biggest threat, but they believe this is the way the world works, and it is not worth giving up the power and benefits they gain from it—a casualty in war. The funny way life works is that society teaches us the men who do defend and protect women are pussies, and they are often referred to as the hood's most infamous "Captain Save a Hoe." Some men do not speak up for women out of fear of being made fun of and looking fragile—fear of retaliation and physical harm. Women know all too well the violence that comes with standing up to sexist dudes. This is usually why we remain silent or laugh to ease our anxiety; so many women have been killed for less. For walking away, ignoring or saying no. It is statistically proven that when men are pulled aside by other men they respect, they change their behaviors or language for the better. Most guys perform for their friends and what they might presume to be cool or not. So in summary, men listen to other men. Women cannot gain true equality when half of the population is making a punchline out of our pain. It is time to put on your big boy boots, take accountability, and hold those up around you to that same standard. You can no longer afford the luxury of standing by and letting sickos get away with things you know are not ok. It might mean losing a friend because of his dealings with underage women or friends who you know physically abuse their girlfriends. Yes, it is time to get *that* uncomfortable and not because your mom is the most amazing woman in the world, not because you have sisters, or a daughter on the way, but because women are humans and count as the other half of the world. Respect for women should not be warranted only for the ones whom you love, are related to, or find attractive. We have to remember that silence is an insidious enemy, so when you see a woman being abused, intimidated, or assaulted, step in. Men also must create a space among each other that allows them to be open, honest, and vulnerable because having friends you cannot speak to when you are facing issues out of fear of ridicule does not help. Excessive partying, drinking, smoking, sex, or video games can result in covering your wounds with vices and will only prolong your issues. It is amazing to have friends with whom you can celebrate life and have fun with but make sure they are just as eager to sit in silence with you when you are going through it. Friends who pick up your favorite things when you feel like staying inside or answer your calls when you really need them and not just for a night out. Remember that men die at alarming rates due to suicide, so it is time you start giving each other spaces to be vulnerable and honest. To be able to catch them when they are drifting and sit them down when they are going down destructive paths, or just letting your guard down so they can be comfortable doing the same. If you never had these kinds of men in your life growing up, you know how hard life can be. So become that man for the younger ones; take young men under your wing and guide them because if you do not, somebody else will. On the team for true liberation, we are all on the same side, but you cannot be for true freedom if you do not want to see us all on an even playing field. Some can confuse this with wanting the same power as white men or being able to inflict pain and get away with the same atrocities because for them, this is what an even playing field looks like. I never want to see a world where rapists walk freely in the name of equality. When we talk about the pain we have experienced at the hands of men, it is not to drive a wedge or to be divisive. We have marched for you. We have cried for you. We have bled for you. We have died for you. We are taught that the more pain we can take, the stronger and better women we are. We have protected the hands that abused us because to call the cops on our men is to be on the oppressors' side. We know the disadvantage of black and brown bodies in the prison system, and they have used this against us in exchange for silence. We will no longer protect you at our own expense. The time to stand up for each other is now.

CHAPTER 9
Forcing an Island:
Hypocrisy at Our Alters

There is something about the Caribbean, its elders and the prayers that come from them that feel different from anything you could find now. In my home, it was normal to wake up at 2 in the morning with droplets of water hitting your face. When we were kids, my mom made it her mission every night to walk over to us and say a quick prayer over us as we slept. When she finished praying, she would sprinkle holy water on us and touch us with the sign of the cross. *"Que Dios me lo protege."* May God protect you. As a child, the first few times it happened, I was absolutely mortified. I watched too many scary movies as a kid to wake up to a random figure in a corner praying over me in a foreign language, but eventually I began to feel a certain peace everywhere I went. I learned that even in my most vulnerable moments, my mom was up protecting us. This latched on to me unconsciously because as a child I began to enter every room in my home before I went to bed for a prayer and the sign of the cross to protect the person sleeping in that room. I did this with every room in the house and even remember taking these prayers to my windows to toss them into the sky for the rest of my family who were at their own homes to receive.

As an adult, I look back at this innocent thought process and see how easily what you see is what you become. Without ever noticing, I had followed my mother's footsteps because of the love and protection she had prayed over me. These prayers are still working over time and protecting me to this day. In my culture they say if you really need something, ask your elders to pray for you. They have God on speed dial, and he never lets it ring more than once. I grew up in an extremely religious but united family. Tuesdays and Thursdays were for Bible study and teen-led church groups; Sundays were spent with the family right after mass, and Saturday mornings consisted of us dragging ourselves out of bed for communion classes while cursing our parents in our heads for taking away our sleep. Every other weekday we prayed the rosary as a unit in our homes as most of the people in my family were parishioners of the church and servers in the community. We were raised with rules and many restrictions regarding what we were allowed to do, wear, listen to, or act like, but we had a lot of more freedom compared to other kids. Many were under strict dress codes and restrictions that allowed them no control over their lives.

Growing up, I had never met a Dominican who was not Catholic, and it wasn't normal for others to learn

about religions outside of it, never mind even think-
ing about exploring them. As I grew up, traveled, and
met different people, I began to learn and look into
other religions because I was fascinated that although
everybody had their own customs and way of moving
throughout this world, we somehow all aligned in one
way—faith. I began to notice the trend of restraint and
militant ways of the older generation in my culture
when I would question traditional customs and damaging rhetoric. I researched the lack of liberty and freedom in our island and how many of the enslaved
people who were forcefully brought from West Africa
came bearing their own cultures, religion, and language. At first, the Spaniards did not understand it
and were terrified of everything that was different from
theirs, but they let them practice it on the island until
they believed it was building unity. Then they banned
their traditions and way of praying because they felt it
would eventually result in mass slave revolts. This religion was called Voodoo. Now the origins of Voodoo
are not as sinister as they have been portrayed, so I was
astounded when I found the similarities to Catholicism.
We praised through singing, dancing, and drumming,
we caught the Holy Spirit, spoke in tongues, and drank
the blood of Jesus. While every religion has people
who use practices for evil and personal gain, Voodoo
has been extremely demonized because of these few. If
you pay close attention, you will see it is mostly rooted
in racism, and in my island this disdain stems from the
Spaniards forcing the Catholic religion onto ours while
making sure other practicing religions had to convert

or were thrown off of the island. One of the biggest documented *mojones* ever, Trujillo had forced himself between the church and state when he became the dictator of the Dominican Republic. The more I learned, the more it began to make so much sense as to why our culture was the way it was in church.

When I entered my teenage years, we were sent off to weekend retreats with 100 other kids where they discussed passages from the Bible, abstinence, homosexuality, marriage, sex, and abortion. We were coming into the age of understanding as teenagers and needed to begin learning about this information. The problem was they used fear and lies to instill terror into us. In my church they used God as a weapon as to why we should follow rules. They portrayed him as someone who was waiting for you to die so he could fry your ass up, not as someone who wanted to love and protect you. These weekend retreats consisted of us being taught a few great things like passages and lessons in the Bible, how to heal, and how to get out of addiction or emotional turmoil. They also really wanted you to know how deep in hell your cell would be if you were gay and how fast your organs would fall out of your ass if you had premarital sex. How alcohol was the devil's piss and marijuana was grown from the devil's garden, but still one of the most vivid things I remember was the topic of abortion. They spent an entire day showing graphic pictures and explaining how the devil had his hands in our vaginas. They went on a 6-hour teaching tour as to why women were murderers if they decided to terminate a pregnancy and how a baby made from rape was God's gift to you, and you were to accept it as a blessing. As someone who was experiencing sexual assault at that exact age, I could not for the life of me understand why they were allowed to have microphones. Had they ever been assaulted or taken advantage of? Were they ever raped? Had they experienced years of disgust and blame? The change that happens in your body and soul? The distrust you have in the world afterwards? They told us why they wanted laws in place to protect the cells of a baby, but I could not help but think of the actual living women they were neglecting. Why should my personal decision give me authority over the woman sitting next to me as if our stories were the same?

The older I got, the more I decided to learn about laws made against women. While I knew of the racism Margaret Sanger had led her programs with, I grew up to be pro-choice. I wanted women to have the final decision over what happened to their bodies, which in Santo Domingo translates to you being a *bruja*. Not really, but that is how they will treat you. I felt guilty as a teenager about the lies that I had been taught, but eventually I learned that to be pro-choice means to give women 100 per cent control over their own bodies, regardless of your personal beliefs or opinions. I still cannot grasp why this is a debate among politicians. Old white men should not be able to pass laws regarding women who could be their granddaughters. The politicians who believe fetuses and cells deserve more rights than the women carrying them are the same ones who are flying their mistresses into Canada to terminate pregnancies made outside of their marriages. This is not even a dig, but factual—look it up. Our politicians are notorious for being anti-abortion and anti-homosexuality while practicing both behind closed doors. The bottom line is some women want children; some do not. Some want children, but just not right now. Some women have been raped or are in terrible living conditions, and some women are suffering with mental health issues or are in abusive relationships they are fighting to get out of. Some women have a high possibility that her child or both of them could die during birth, but none of these are your business. To be a feminist means to be pro-choice and give women the space to choose what is right for them. We respect whatever decision you make because it was yours, and it is not fair to bring our religious beliefs into politics as not everyone follows the same traditions or has the same values. You never have to imagine an America where Muslims try to ban bacon or where Mormons try to ban coffee, but for some reason, Christians and Catholics are notorious for wanting to put our personal religious beliefs into politics that affect everybody. It is also comical to have a Bible full of rules and things you should not be doing then picking 10 out of 300 things to focus on because they do not personally pertain to you. You must follow your faith with love and acceptance of others and their faiths. Mind your body; mind your business.

These opinions in religion and choice can cause a real drift in our relationships with the older generations. For most young adults who were raised in extremely religious Christian and Catholic homes, our relationship with the church has suffered and ultimately so has our relationship with God. I can speak for myself when I say as a young girl, I became resentful seeing the hypocrisy in our churches and the people running them. Many of us watched greedy churches prey on people's need for financial gain, normalized pedophilia and abusive leaders in our church, while some of us watched our parents drink themselves into a rage and indulge in infidelity, physical or sexual abuse, lying, stealing, and worse. They cleaned up and sat in silence for two hours on a Sunday morning, and all sins were suddenly forgiven. We watched pastors have children outside of their marriages and be accused of rape or molestation, and then we watched our communities cover them in prayer while leaving the little boys and girls they had abused to live in silence and shame. Our communities are known for protecting pedophiles as many believe they are still children of God and must be prayed over to be cured of this sickness. They are allowed to roam freely with children and are never charged, multiplying the pain throughout the years. This is not only in the church but in our families as well, as we all have the family creeps. The one who causes all the women to put on extra layers of clothes as soon as they hear they're coming around. They are at every family cookout and holiday party, comfortable, happy, fed, and loved, while there is a child sitting near whose life has been filled with anxiety and depression while being neglected and unprotected by these same people. We shun and shame our gay family members or those who do not fit in a box while forming prayer circles around pedophiles. I did not notice it until I was an adult, but I resented churches because of the people running them. Unbeknownst to me, I let this affect my relationship with God. It took many years of repairing and unlearning what I was taught to be able to be vulnerable enough to begin rebuilding my relationship with God. I realized I could talk to God anytime I wanted. I did not have to put on my Sunday best or have my hair intact, and I did not have to sit with people I did not trust. I realized he was not a scary man micromanaging my every step from the sky but someone I could talk to at any time as if he were a trusted friend. I know now that I had to experience those things because the bond I formed from my internal work and healing made it so much more special this way. For me the guidance that comes from within is directly from him. I know this because writing was never in my mind, and I never dreamed of being an author; I just had a message that was pouring out of me that I desperately needed to release. The universe made me feel as if I had no choice, but now I know that it was God guiding me from within. It is why you are reading this today. Your relationship with God and whichever religion you choose to live in should be yours, not whatever was passed down through generations or what your grandmother told you about her relationship with it. Question your customs and ask the right questions; form your own relationship if this is what you want, and watch the new world that opens when you have a faith you truly believe in.

CHAPTER 10
Three Headed Dragon:
Self Worth, Love, and Respect

If we can arm the younger generation with tools on confidence and how to conquer self-doubt, we can shield them from the many things we have gone through as adults. We can build an extremely powerful generation with high levels of confidence if we can teach them early how to accept and love themselves in all totality and how to remove the shame from their flaws and instead move into accepting the beauty of individuality. There are so many layers that contribute to destruction of our childlike enthusiasm as we grow into adults. Unfortunately, by the time some of us have reached the "real world," we have been beaten into submission by society, friends, and extremely negative family upbringings. So many do not get the chance to figure out who they are because they are told what they are supposed to be. Until you grow up and leave these environments, fear has been instilled so deeply you never open yourself up to the world. From the moment you turn on the television, you see constant advertisements telling you what you need to look like, buy, and wear to be worthy of respect. You can be raised in a family who is extremely vile and project their flaws, standards, and views onto your life. This looks different for everybody because we all come from different places and lead different lives. We each have our personal preferences, and we all explore different religions and languages; while we experience this form of brainwashing differently, it will show up in our lives the same—in shame, self-doubt, and a lack of confidence.

For men, the most common form of attack is their manhood. As a boy, you are bombarded with a set list of what it is to be a "real" man. You are not allowed to feel, care, or live your life according to your own rules as to what you believe manhood means to you personally. For your "man-membership" to be approved, you need to deny things that bring you joy, internalize all of your pain, and accumulate the estate of Bill Gates by 19 so you can deserve access to friends who look up to you and women who would die to stand next to you. If you cannot fulfill these tasks as an adult man, you are presumed to be dead. For women, these advertisements come in the form of beauty standards. You need to have the shape of a Coke bottle, porcelain-like skin, and live your life as a true doll. The most important part about being a Barbie is looking beautiful. A closed mouth is more important than anything you can put on, so shut the fuck up, please. These standards get more violent the more marginalized you are. If you are black, you are constantly bombarded with assimilation tactics from lightening creams to hair relaxers. Everywhere you turn there is somebody telling you that you are too dark, your hair is too nappy, your features are too loud, and your culture is too scary. Society caters to a racist system that upholds European beauty standards and is made with the intention of per-suading minorities to unconsciously believe they are less than by simply being born different. These assimi-lation tactics are made to make you feel like your skin, hair, and culture is somehow dirty and dangerous. This unconsciously teaches black children everywhere that the closer in proximity you are to whiteness, the more beautiful and successful you can be. If you are a fat woman, the ghost of Future will visit you twice a month and whisper, "you are not getting into heaven until you drop 50 pounds, bitch." Women are picked apart literally from head to toe by their families and then followed by the pressures of society if you do not fit into the mold of what they deem to be acceptable. Constant pressure from everything around you can kill your confidence before you even know what it is. Can you imagine being picked apart for the way you look, who you love, or the way your culture is celebrated? This is what I mean by our experiences all being differ-ent. As a white woman, you may understand what it is like to feel the pressure of sexism, but you will never understand what it is like to be a woman of color and have racism thrown in the mix with sexism. We must acknowledge that some people are chastised and more violently presented than others. Now if you cannot acquire these material items or become this impossible blow-up doll, you are deemed unworthy of basic love and respect.

Another form of feelings of unworthiness can stem from issues with our educational system. Our schools teach us that we are measured by our grades, how well we remember false history, and how fast we can multiply. These generic and basic questions, that really do not matter, are what they judge your intelligence and capability on for the rest of your life. If you are not someone who works well with others or is good under pressure, you will not feel smart or capable in these environments. Sometimes you can take this feeling of unworthiness into an area where you can captivate and conquer. If you have toxic parents or family members who have spent a lifetime trying to motivate you by comparing you to others, constantly nit picking about how you look, how you choose to dress, where you work, or all things that make you *you*, this can result in another form of anxiety and self-doubt that can build inside of you because of it. Sometimes we dive into our churches and religion to seek help. These too, if led by the wrong people, can become avenues of shame, silence, and sadness. If your pastor preaches about your sins and why you will be cast into hell more than shouting about your greatness and how you are a child of God, who always forgives and knows you are deserving of a beautiful life, you might be going to the wrong church, as I was.

Social media is a fairly new form of entertainment that is accelerating anxiety and body dysmorphia by 15 years. The standards get more unrealistic, and the audience gets much younger. Five-year-olds should not care about their thighs. Your personal trials like experiencing sexual assault, racism, rape, homophobia, childhood traumas, and other lingering issues are something we need to dissect and come to terms with because these are all things that make you feel small, unimportant, and as if nothing you do really matters. We all have a huge weight on our shoulders trying to uphold outdated standards, and none of us would like to keep up with them. I truly believe that the best way to build our youths' self-esteem and rebuild our own is to conquer the three-headed dragon. self- worth, self-love, and self-respect. I have come to the conclusion that these are the three major compartments in living a confident and beautiful life that allow you to give fully to others while keeping your values and standards. Let's get into the differences:

SELF-WORTH

Your past pains, traumas, and mistakes can trick you into believing that you do not deserve love, respect, happiness, and sometimes even wealth. To have true self-worth means to forgive yourself for all of your past mistakes. This goes deeper than we may think, as most of these things can stem from our childhood or early adult life. We really need to dig in deep to find these things that are holding us back mentally. Since our brain remembers every single mistake we have made, it can trick your mind into believing that you do not deserve to live a great life. Our mind often wanders back to places nobody else remembers, but you do—even if it was for two seconds in 1998, you remember vividly. Sometimes we can take a small, bad moment and turn it into a long, bad life. We still think these minor issues are defining factors as to how people will view and treat us. Fortunately, people do not have binoculars that can see your past, so we only see you in the now—as terrifying and beautiful as that can be. None of us is perfect and all have our past faults, but we are also our toughest critics. We let the external small things of our past dictate what we feel we deserve now. So even if you love how you look, are excited and passionate about your career, and thriving in every other aspect of your life, if you still have underlying guilt and unworthiness, it will show in your life choices, and you will not be able to experience true joy. Especially your choices in men, women, or friends. These moments range according to how we feel at a certain moment in our lives. Feeling unworthy can be dangerous as it leads to vices and destructive behavior. For you to move past this sense of worthlessness, you must be brutally honest with yourself. The uncomfortable kind of honest—you know the kind—the kind that makes you angry, defensive, and sad. Only you know that thing that lives in the back of your head, so nobody can heal it but you. It is up to you to allow yourself to feel the pain and forgive yourself for the reaction. Feel the sadness, anger, hurt, and betrayal, then give yourself the same compassion you would give to your best friend. Accept that these things affected your decisions and led you to behave destructively. You hurt people you loved and yourself in the process. Nobody is perfect but this does not mean you need to wallow in sadness because of your past. While you should shield and protect yourself, you must make sure you are not running from healthy relationships, wonderful opportunities, or material items you feel as if you do not deserve. You can love how you look, what you do, and what you bring to this world, but if you feel like you should still be paying for your mistakes, it will show up in your life choices. You will continue to choose low hanging fruit because of what is available.

SELF-LOVE

The revolutionary act of resistance is you loving and accepting your physical form in your entirety. It is hard to accept yourself in a world that is constantly changing and telling you, you are not enough. By the time you are ten you have seen thousands of ads telling you why you are simply garbage. You can't get that job because you don't know how to dress; your crush does not like you because of the pimple on your cheek. They want you to believe your life will be full of misery if you do not fit into these molds. These are just some of the methods they use to wheel you in with things that can trigger your insecurities, just so they have customers indebted to changing their every way of being until they eventually die. They have painted a specific picture of what a woman should be, and then marketed billions of products to convince us there is something wrong with us. They trick us into believing we are here for the consumption of others. We are taught to compete with people through looks, material items, partners, or attention. This creates a damaging self-esteem for young girls and unrealistic standards for boys. We become shy, timid, and passive women who don't let themselves shine due to crippling self-consciousness. They try to dim our identities so they can turn our worth into something you can buy on sale at a store— except the look is always changing so you will always be chasing something different. To have unfiltered and unconditional self-love is to say you choose you in all aspects over society's beauty standards and over your family and friends' thoughts of you. You choose yourself over the pressures of this world to conform to what they think is supposed to be you. Giving up the "what ifs" of complete strangers to your personal "oh well." The pressures we face as humans for existing in the skin you were born in can be extremely crippling. Low confidence can become body dysmorphia if you have internalized these things about yourself and do not tackle them early on. From your hair texture, weight, scars or arms, the pitch of your voice and shape of your nose, we all have our own insecurities and things we have been taught to hate. Throughout the years we began to nitpick at ourselves. We begin to look at ourselves through the eyes of others and the projections they put on us. These can be small moments that happened as children that we carry throughout our adult lives. This insecurity can be something that the outside world does not even notice or care about. It is not about them but about how you have internalized what you feel you are "supposed" to look like. This can stop you from doing regular day to day activities such as going to the beach, networking, and denying amazing opportunities that you talk yourself out of. The pressures of social media have enhanced these things as we are seeing so many unnatural air-brushed images of people who do not look like this in real time. We must learn to accept everything that we cannot fix because even surgery can become a vice. Running from things that are inside will leave you exhausted. You can change your toxic patterns and behavior, but you must first learn to see yourself through your own eyes and not through society's goggles. Learn to see yourself in the face that lights up when you talk about your passion. The body that fights every single day to keep you alive and has succeeded through a global pandemic. The voice you hate that shakes rooms when you speak. The jiggly arms that won't hesitate to feed a stranger and simultaneously punch someone's lights out to protect your loved ones. It is an everyday fight and something you need to remind yourself of constantly. While this is always easier said than done, you can start today. This means listening to words of affirmation. Speaking life into yourself—out loud, even if you feel weird about it at first. We have said so many mean things that our spirits react shockingly when we speak life into ourselves. You will be able to see the difference in your immediate reaction. Be patient with yourself. I learned that the first thing that comes to your mind is what you have been taught and programmed by society, and the second thought is who you really are or are trying to elevate into becoming. So even if you think to yourself something negative, counter it with something positive. Give yourself time to adjust, as you have said or thought at least one negative thing about yourself every single day since you felt what insecurity was. We must set out to understand that as cliché as it sounds, what you do for this world and how you treat people are the only things that ultimately matter when it is all said and done. The exterior is just the physical, but you are what you do, say, and create. Do not fall into the traps of this world because you will never be satisfied; they will not be either. Instead tell yourself how grateful you are to have a working mind that allows you to grow. Pick up books; listen to a podcast; follow women and men who support messages of love and acceptance in our community. Leave people who constantly promote perfection and make you feel worse. Talk about your insecurities to your closest and trusted friends and make a conscious decision to speak life into yourself. Be patient—it is worth it.

SELF-RESPECT

Self-respect is one of the main ingredients in having a life where you can give freely without people taking advantage of you. This is the final layer because for me, it is the most important. As a young girl, I let the world run me mad. As a woman, I needed to create boundaries. This does not mean you let the world turn you cold. It means you shine for others, but still allow yourself time to recharge. It means you put your needs first, and then you can move onto your loved ones; you cannot help anybody when you are running dry, depressed, anxious, or upset. Many things like our past mistakes and things we have let people get away with can ultimately cut our self-respect down from short to non-existent. The first step to rebuilding the trust in yourself is to forgive yourself—for your past mistakes, for not knowing better or knowing better but doing differently. Count it as a lesson, charge it to the game, and promise yourself you will never allow these things to happen again. Don't be so hard on yourself, but realize how your past has led you to this very moment. Next, it is extremely important to know in full detail what you want out of this life, what you will allow, and what you will stand and fight for. You must have a code of ethics, morals, and values that you stand by, especially when nobody else is watching. Some of these can stem from your family and their traditions. You can keep these if they still align with you, but I want you to make a list of your own, and if you don't know where to start, that is okay. I did not sit down until I was 21 years old and wrote my own set of values and things that I felt guided my spirit. Gift yourself with an hour of silence and think to yourself what you would like your legacy to be. Here is mine:

- Love on your folks but hold them accountable.
- Never count favors.
- Leave people feeling better than before they met me.
- Never do anything expecting something in return.
- Treat every person regardless of status with respect.
- Speak my truth no matter how terrified I am.
- Criticize and correct those you love in private.
- Love yourself but admit your shortcomings. Commit to change.
- Stand up for those who can't stand up for themselves.
- Time for yourself is time for yourself. Do not bargain.
- Don't let people waste your time.
- Pay attention to what they do, not what they say.

My list has grown and changed throughout the years, just as I have. Yours will too. Some you can keep private or change if you feel you need to. The most important part is what you require from others, you must bring yourself. I ask of my loved ones what I lead my life by. As you grow up and face different challenges, you will learn more and more about what upsets or brightens your spirit and what you simply will not tolerate. Just ask yourself the right questions. What would you like your legacy to be? Do you want to live a fulfilled life or would you like to just exist and avoid all happiness and sadness? I want you to use the word NO—a luxury you feel you never deserved. I want you to set boundaries for yourself and get rid of any people in your life who feel attacked by your growth. I want you to trust your mind and intuition enough to make your own decisions. I do not want you to look left or right to familiar faces when deciding what is best for your life. I want you to know what you offer and bring to this world, and create boundaries to protect it. Cut ties with those who disrespect and disregard you. The people who treat you like a burden and do not work on themselves to be better do not deserve to have access to you. You need to understand this because God will not bring you what you truly deserve and are asking for if you have seat fillers in your section. I want you to do what is right when nobody is watching. Do not let people talk you out of your ideas and decisions. I want you to choose yourself first and leave things that do not honor you, may it be a relationship, a friend, family member, or a fuck ass job. I do not want you to fall into the trap of lowering your standards because they talk you down a good one. Do not let people come into your life and distract you from your life's mission. Let them find a clown for their circus somewhere else. Form your own opinions; look into yourself for answers. When you begin to tolerate things, people become comfortable in what you choose to accept from them. Takers do not know when to stop taking, so givers need to know when to stop giving. You must assert yourself and stop worrying about what outsiders think of your decisions or ideas. Breaking free from the shackles of criticism will change your life. Develop a filter, one that takes advice but drains people's motives from it. You can listen to your loved ones, but that does not mean you get to internalize it. Take everything with a grain of salt. You regain your control and can listen to what others say without making this your reality. Respect for yourself gives you a different kind of God-sent confidence. Stand your ground; it does not mean to be vicious but to own your power and life. You can be a delicate, flowery, dangerous bitch too. Do not let people mess with you. There are many layers to confidence, which is why some women, who are intelligent, passionate, and confident in work or physicality, may have chaotic relationships at home. They can have it all together but still feel as if they do not deserve the things they have or want because they still think badly of themselves. Some people are amazing but let others walk all over them. We all have different avenues of where we should work on, but when you gather all three levels, you become the supreme power-puff bitch in charge. The point is to walk through all of your underlying issues with yourself. We all have different struggles and upbringings, and your childhood has a lot to do with the way you perceive yourself and move throughout this world. So, if you can remove the goggles the world has placed on you so you can look through your own eyes and see yourself for the true work of art that you are, it can be magical. You have overcome the biggest obstacles, fought your way through life, been attacked from every angle from strangers to your closest kin, said the worst of words, and been alone in a room full of people. Only you know what you have been through, but this is a start: acknowledging your pain and suffering, and doing the dirty work to dig yourself out of the mud. The world shines much brighter on this side. We welcome you with open arms! I'm still digging myself through the mud, so if you catch me lacking, God is still working on me. You no longer have to punish yourself for your past. Understand that you are worthy of existing; you deserve to be here, to conquer your dreams, fall deep into love, and raise a generation that does not need to heal from low confidence and insecurities. (If you want to...) Let go of what you *think* you should look, act, and talk like. Embrace who you are, even the things you hate the most. Give yourself the support you give your best friend when they are in a time of need. Pour yourself a glass and work through it, bitch! I love you.

CHAPTER 11
The Beauty in Evil:
Holding Women Accountable

There is a layer of protection for women who are predators that does not allow us to see them as what they are: destructive. Men who are victims of sexual abuse are usually forced into silence because of the shame and ridicule. Although it is a very taboo subject, one out of four men will experience some type of sexual or physical assault in their lifetime. Very early in life, boys are taught what the definition of a man is: an alpha male with dominant traits. While there are many great things to come from having a driven personality, it does not allow space for a man to heal from those things that have hurt him because the "alpha male" can never see himself as a victim. They are taught to take everything to the chest and throw it to the back of their minds because that is what men are supposed do. Boys who experience physical abuse are usually laughed at because society cannot understand why they could not defend themselves, even though society also told them that adults know what is best and to never put their hands on women. Men who report domestic violence are almost never taken seriously, which has become an incredibly serious issue as women can be verbally, physically, and emotionally abusive in relationships, friendships, and at work. For many millennial men, it is normal to be in a relationship where they are on the receiving end of controlling issues. They stay with women who are extremely insecure and emotionally abusive who believe that denying men the rights to see their family and friends, or having a life outside of them is somehow love and protection. Controlling women believe that due to the man's past issues or insecurities they can use this form of mental manipulation to invade his privacy and overstep his boundaries to keep men under supervision. We live in a weird time when things like possessiveness and physical violence are looked at as traits of someone who really cares about you. People who have no self-control or respect for you are being loved on even more. This is extremely backwards and has many people staying in relationships they should be running from. There are poisonous mothers who have not healed from their own wounds and are taking it out daily on their children with mistreatment, neglect, physical, verbal, or sexual abuse that builds an immense kind of trauma.

Historically, feminism has acknowledged the role of dangerous women and how many can be rapists, pedophiles, and murderers while sitting behind pretty faces and innocent eyes. Since we are taught that pedophiles and murderers are usually strange men in trench coats, women can use their likability to wheel you in.

There are many women just like Ghislaine Maxwell (who will probably have committed the strangest of "suicides" by the time this book is published) out there. These are the kinds of women who know that we feel protected by them and use it to their advantage. I have to say these are the worst kind of women, the ones who crave the dominance and power evil men have to the point that they will put their own in harm's way—women who want to be a part of the big boys club so bad they will disrespect, hurt, manipulate, and even kill other women.

White feminism teaches you to want a seat at the table, even if it is built on the backs of Native and Black women. I have no interest in having inclusiveness in destruction because this to me is not equality. I have nothing in common with women who do not want to see us all on an equal playing field but instead want the same demonic power old white men hold. This is a privilege afforded to few women, as we know the weight white women's tears hold. You do not have to do much research to learn of the millions lynched, burned, and jailed behind the lies of white women, women who were never held accountable because the blood was not physically on their hands. There is no moral ground for women whose fight for rights includes being able to join the KKK and terrorize the rest of us in the name of equal opportunity—fuck you forever.

Now, of course, seeing women in positions of power in important places is inspiring and beautiful. We feel a sense of relief when we step into each other's spaces because we understand what it feels like to be in male-dominated industries. Sometimes you meet incredible women who are welcoming, inclusive, and really want to see you win. They make sure to build you up; they make space for you and help you win in any way they can. This is one of the most refreshing and beautiful feelings of sisterhood: we look out for and protect each other. Sometimes when you get closer, however, you might meet women who have complete disdain and hate for other women. Since we are nitpicked and torn apart from head to toe all of our lives, some women might begin to inflict this same treatment on other women. We begin to adopt sexist theories about ourselves and project them onto other women. Since society teaches us that women are catty, stupid, irrational, and annoying, we internalize sexism and try to separate ourselves from other women. This cycle can look like you've decided to only have male friends because of the stereotypes surrounding women. Now this does not mean there is something wrong with you just because you have male friends, but that there is something wrong if you cannot give women chances because you are judging and projecting onto them what you were taught. Being resentful, jealous, and spiteful, denying women opportunities, refusing access to things that can help them and their careers, slut shaming, reinforcing negative stereotypes about women, and victim blaming are all tactics developed under internalized sexism. You begin to believe being irrational, mentally under-developed, and a victim are women characteristics so instead of opening the door and allowing in the ones to come after us, you slam it shut. The portrayal of power is to be assertive, to dominate, to be egotistical, loud, to intimidate, and to take up space, and many women believe adopting these traits is what will get them ahead—and it will, to an extent. But when you catch yourself inflicting the same pain you were put through out of resentment, you have chosen the wrong direction.

It is extremely important to note the role of dangerous women throughout history. This means having an honest conversation about mothers and caregivers who have been extremely vile and abusive towards children, pedophiles who need to be registered as offenders, women who physically and verbally assault their partners, and the white dangerous women of the world who have caused havoc and pain in the black community. I do not want to live in a world where people think freedom means everybody gets a piece of corruption or a "get out of jail free" card. I would rather it all collapse before we build equality on a false foundation.

CHAPTER 12
Red Light, Green Light: One, Two, Three

M anipulation is one of the first forms of abuse in almost any physically violent relationship. This can vary in all of your relationships with your parents, employers, siblings, and even the government officials and politicians who are elected in your town. They all have the same common goal: get what they want out of you by any means necessary. They are avid listeners because they want to get you to talk long enough to reveal vulnerable information, which they will later use against you. Manipulation is an incredibly evil behavior that can be learned when dealing with narcissistic parents or caregivers who used it against you when you were young. If as a child, the adults in your life made you feel like you were insufficient or made you compete for love, money, or affection, you could have become used to the feeling of worthlessness. These children eventually grow up to be adults who feel like they do not have control or influence, so they begin to do destructive things to accumulate it by any means necessary. This tactic stems from feeling inadequate, and it can prompt a never-ending craving for power and control.

It is incredibly important for you to note the characteristics and the reoccurring themes of each person you come in contact with because the things they may want from you could include money, sex, attention, physical affection, association, sympathy, material items, or other things that are not tangible. It can happen in a relationship with your girlfriend or boyfriend, who can use your flaws, mistakes, and, ultimately, the love you have for them against you. Politicians use this as a means to exploit your pain and vulnerabilities for their own profits and to get their personal agenda across to be voted into office. They run campaigns based on what is trending at the moment, use sensitive points, and jump into whatever and whoever is the majority. They have no grounded values or morals; they only want to win.

It can happen at work with a boss who wants to make you do things outside of your job description. Some do not want you to leave but will not meet the requirements you need to stay; they believe if they beat your confidence to the ground, you will eventually think that you are lucky to even be there. I once worked for a man who would ask his employees deep and personal questions as an act of bonding, just to bring them up when he needed something from them or if they threatened to leave. If you mentioned that your mom was sick and it was tough on your family, he would keep that locked away in his bucket of bitch until you tried to quit or questioned his methods. Then he would bring up your mother's pain and how you would not be able to afford being without a job for too long. (And he always wondered why I never spoke to him.)

Parents, on the other hand, are notorious for using manipulation to get sympathy or favors from their children. They take advantage of the love you have for them and use the things they have done for you, to manipulate you into doing things you do not want to do.

Nothing makes me happier than shielding amazing people from the leeches of this world, so I want to help you discover any existing predators in your life and protect you from future ones. I have compiled a list of red flags you should always take note of, but remember: manipulators do not appear out of thin air but in subtle hints as they ease their way into your mind by getting your trust first.

Let's get into it.

RED FLAGS:

- Completely disregards your personal boundaries.
- Invalidates your experiences or points of view.
- Has an extreme fear of losing you and does outrageous things to test this.
- Pressures you to have sex or things you are not comfortable with.
- Is overly critical of you. Nitpicks at your looks, personality, or art.

- Lacks empathy.
- Is hyper focused on your relationship extremely early; has no outside life or responsibilities.
- Over shares in hopes of receiving vital information from you.
- Avoids conflicts and is passive aggressive.
- Gets offended when you make decisions for yourself.
- Possessive; extremely jealous and controlling.
- Coerces you into doing things you do not want to do.
- Gives you no privacy or personal space.
- Blames you for "pushing" them into their violent outbursts.
- Intimidates you purposely.
- Disrespects you out loud; apologizes in private.
- Extremely hostile, angry, and dark spirited whenever you are happy.
- Makes a mockery of your weaknesses and insecurities.
- Talks over you to silence you.
- Makes you feel as if you are stupid or unattractive.
- Uses time against you and gives you ultimatums.
- They lie unprovoked, are deceptive, and have mastered the art of blaming everyone else to dodge all responsibility.
- It is always made about them—even when it is not.

These are just some of the things you can look out for when protecting your energy and your space. Manipulators are usually some of the nicest people you will meet. They get inside your space to gain your trust, then begin using your weaknesses or vulnerabilities against you. Many people cannot see these things when they are happening, and it is not because you are weak but because they get your trust or catch you in a vulnerable state. They are also incredibly notorious for treating you like Future but acting like Russell in front of your friends and family, so most people will never understand the evil you see. They know very well what they are doing: performing. They will compliment and disrespect you in the same sentence, and eventually you will start to look at yourself through their eyes. They will tell you your dreams are great but poke holes in your confidence and question your ability to get it done. This will destroy your belief in yourself. They will call your passions and opinions silly; eventually you will stop saying them out loud for fear of ridicule and laughter. They have stolen your voice. They will shout out your flaws and whisper your greatness. They will convince you that your standards are too high so you will stop asking for what you deserve. They will bring up the faults in your family and friends and why they are no good; little by little you will begin to see them less. They finally have you isolated, and now nobody will be able to remind you how much better you deserve. They can talk you out of progressing financially, physically, and mentally out of fear of you outgrowing them and realizing how much better you deserve. When you begin to believe what they say about you and have come under their control, you cannot leave, talk, or eat without their permission. They will answer questions meant for you and act as if you are their property. They will talk over you constantly, question your intelligence, and overpower you as a silencing tactic because they believe they have worked far too hard for you to be your own person. Some people may believe this is normal, that relationships come with compromises and sacrifices, and while this is true, these sacrifices should not come with the cost of the things that bring you joy and happiness. You will notice if you are the only one making adjustments to accommodate at the expense of your own peace or happiness, as abusers love to make people think life centers around them. They want you to believe they are the reason you smile, and they will constantly remind you that anything good about yourself came from them. This is why they try incredibly hard to isolate you from the people and things you love; it is important that your happiness relies solely on them. This is not the same as someone with good intentions who can see people you care about are taking advantage of you or causing you harm. This is why it is very important to work on your emotional intelligence so you can choose for yourself what is best for your life and make sure nobody is taking advantage of you.

Another violent form of manipulation is called gas lighting, when somebody tries to use your memory and your own mind against you. They use misinformation, contradiction, and denial to get you to depend on them and their word entirely. This happens when a manipulator has dug their fangs so deeply into your spirit that after years you begin to believe them over your own eyes, ears, and memory. They will say asinine and abusive things and when confronted about it, they will simply accuse you of making it up, overreacting, or being sensitive. They can be caught in dead lies and will convince you so well that you are crazy and that they never did anything of the sort. For children who have abusive parents, when you confront them or try to address the things you went through as a child, you may be met with a completely different story than what you remember. It is very hard for them to admit where they had been lacking and did not do their part in making you feel safe, so they would rather deny it ever happened. These kinds of people are so persistent in what they are saying that you can actually begin to believe you did not hear or see what you did... that maybe you did hear it wrong. Except you didn't. But... maybe you did. But it can't possibly be because you know what you heard. This is the back and forth that can sometimes drive people to lose their minds and question themselves. When you are sure of what you are seeing, hearing, or feeling—never allow anybody to minimize or question this. While you should always allow yourself time to process it, your spirit always knows.

As fast as we should be able to see the many red flags we should avoid, it is equally important to take note of people who are in your life and give you space to grow and thrive. The people who love you unconditionally, the ones who truly want to see you happy and living a joy filled life. Please take note of Green Flags and how to spot the wonderful people in your life who participate in your growth.

GREEN FLAGS

- Give you space to be vulnerable without judgment or ridicule.
- Are self-sufficient. Do not depend only on you for happiness.
- Empathetic to everyone they come across.
- Love to see you win, even if you surpass them.
- Openly communicate without yelling or embarrassing you.
- Honor your boundaries and accept you as a whole person they fortunately get to experience.
- One hand washes the other. You share equal responsibilities in your relationship. There is substantial effort.
- Can look at themselves with honesty and admit when they are at fault. They apologize and fix accordingly.
- Compromise and try to understand the most complicated parts of you.
- Apologize when they are wrong.
- Love on you according to your love language.
- Are interested in your passions and help you with your goals.
- Great listeners. Understand when you need advice and when you need to vent.

- They respect your privacy and individuality.
- They make you feel safe, emotionally and physically.
- You can discuss things freely without fights because you both understand neither of you is the problem. The problem is the problem.

These are some of the key things to look out for when you are meeting new people, and it is why you can meet somebody and simply be drawn to their energy. When you are used to so many negative ways of being shown love, and you learn about the way you have been giving it out yourself, it is important to note that familiarity is the devil's playground. He thrives on the thought that we can become comfortable with pain and sit in sadness because it feels like home. It is almost like when you feel sad and put on a sadder song to make yourself feel worse. We think that if we stay with what we know, we will be all right because at least we know what it feels like. It is important that we do not run from, but *towards* honest and healing love when it shows up. As much pain as there is this world, we must continue to believe in the presence of love and, more importantly, be vulnerable enough to receive it in its totality. Begin the process of slowly removing people from your life who do not serve you a greater purpose and honor those who support your elevation in life. Everybody deserves to live a life with love around them. May we heal our wounds and open the way for the universe to reward us with healthy love by making the right choices.

CHAPTER 13
Dissecting Roles:
Choosing Your Life

One in five women have been beaten by their spouse. One in four women have been sexually abused. Out of the 113 mass shootings that have taken place since 1982, 100 of those were carried out by men. Almost every single one of those mass shooters had a history of domestic violence or assault. There is a conversation to be had around the historical violence of men, but we first need to understand where it begins. There is this misconception that because men have more testosterone, they are just born extremely aggressive and violent. This has been proven to be wrong time and time again. We can see how it starts in our homes, where the stereotypes and gender enforcement first happens. Far before you understand what being a man is you learn through religion, sex, music, television, politics, and sports. They tell you that to be a man is to dominate, to conquer, and overpower. Aggressiveness is your key ingredient. Now while these can be incredible qualities when used for good or when you want to win, they can become destructive very easily.

My older brother is just a barely two years older than me. As kids, when he would cry, he would be met with anger—not from my parents but from older uncles and cousins. He was told how much of a man he was supposed to be and how much of a little girl he was acting like. I did not understand why my sister and I were allowed to cry from a bleeding scraped knee, but somehow the pain my brother felt was less serious because he was born a boy. While we were cared for if we had a bruise, he was told to suck it up. The only emotion boys are allowed to feel publicly is anger because anything else makes you a bitch.

Now if all you see while growing up are the men around you gaining power and respect through destructive ways, especially towards women, you will mirror this and bring it into adult-hood. Boys are not given room to process their emotions so they eventually become soulless men who do not know how or what they feel because they have been taught to push it to the back of their minds all of their lives. There is no such thing as processing it. We teach boys that money is power; it is the defining factor if you are a man or a boy. You aspire your entire life to become wealthy; sometimes it may not even to be financially independent or to build generational wealth, but to fill a void. We teach boys that women are possessions: the more trophies you collect as you go, the more powerful you are. They end up not seeing women as 51 per cent of the population with whom they share this earth, but as things they accumulate and conquer throughout life. You hear it in our music, you watch it on your TV, you see it at school, you indulge in it with porn, you try to rinse it off at church—it lives there too. There is this thing that happens when women begin to talk about the issues they face where a lot of men simply tune out and stop listening. They believe women's issues are women's problems, except that they are not: these are men's issues. When talking about sexual assault or rape against women, we use coded language to negate all responsibility from the attacker and transfer it to the person who was attacked. We have begun blaming women for their own rapes, sexual assaults, and deaths since the first thing we do is ask what they were wearing, why was she with that person, and why was she even outside to begin with. People constantly make excuses for attackers and imply that a woman deserved what was done to her. They say she was raped because she was promiscuous, but we have seen nuns be abused. We hear you blame women for being outside late, yet we see little girls being abused in their homes. The blame that follows a woman after her assault will ensure she never reports it to police or talks about it ever again because she believes she put herself in that position and somehow she deserved it. We have put all the responsibility on women to make sure they cover themselves up, stay inside after 6 p.m., and never go anywhere alone.

We spend years having our daughters run through rape prevention packets and self-defense classes, equipping them with more pepper spray than the NYPD, while simultaneously letting our boys run around freely and chalk up every mistake as "boys will be boys"—not with accountability or words of guidance but as an excuse. Boys need adult men as guides to emotional intelligence and mental support, so they are able to pinpoint what they are feeling, why, and how to move past it. We are human, and while some things come to us naturally, some things you learn as you go. There are incredible positives and negatives to both masculine and feminine traits. There is no right or wrong answer in regards to how you would like to personally lead your life. The beautiful thing about life is you can change and adopt different traits that you feel can bring you happiness and peace. Some of the negative traits regarding masculinity can be unfiltered aggressiveness, being compulsive, egotistical, combative, argumentative, and arrogant. Real masculinity when done right is a beautiful thing to witness. It means to be independent, a leader, self-assured, ambitious, protective, courageous, disciplined, and responsible. You still get to decide what kind of man you want to be without being put in a box made for men who hunted lions with their hands. Trade in the past that you were programmed into for a new and free future. The manliest thing you can do is to stand on your own.

Women can learn so much from the healthy traits of masculinity like being self-assured, independent and courageous. Some of the most damaging traits for women who are feminine can include being extremely passive, codependent, needy, or extremely self-critical. The beautiful thing about being a woman is the compassion, attentiveness, receptiveness, intuition, and empathy that flows through her. In so many ways, women can learn from positive masculine traits on how to grow to be independent and live a life outside of a relationship, putting their dreams, ideas, and happiness first. To follow your heart in becoming a leader and turning up your aggressive side when you need to pull her out to have a word with somebody. You can always keep your grace, but never let people dance on your feet. When you are low on confidence, spike up your arrogance. Remember who are you and what you bring to the table. When you feel arrogant, remember who you were before you knew what you know now. Adjust accordingly. Men can also adopt positive feminine traits that can change their lives and the lives of the people around them. To be compassionate and understanding with those you do not know, to be attentive, patient, and affectionate to your loved ones. Men who have women as friends are statistically more emotionally intelligent and happy. They lead freer lives because they allow themselves to be vulnerable. Get friends who give you the space to heal; it can change your life. There are beautiful qualities in all of us, and to be a truly emotionally healthy individual you can have traits of both masculine and feminine energy inside of you. One will always overpower the other, but the key is to take what you personally need more of. If you have bottled up everything for most of your life, search for your vulnerability and work on it. If you have been defensive and fought your way through everything, find the compassion and let your guard down. Take what you need; leave what you don't. Teach your sons that to be a real man is to be true to yourself. To feel your feelings and pick yourself up when you are ready. To understand that you lose loved ones, go through heartbreaks, and experience physical and emotional pain the same way you do happiness, excitement, and joy. Teach your daughters to be self-sufficient—to understand the power she has and the beauty she brings into the world. To never allow others to lead her off course or take her for granted. The beauty of this life is you always get to choose. The boxes society has built around us are just that, imaginary boxes you can step out of tomorrow if you wanted to—a box that does not give you room to grow because it benefits a system where we all stay in our place. Where men are three times more likely to die from suicide and women die of emotional and physical exhaustion from carrying their families on their back. We are in a new age, and now that we see that stepping out of these boxes is liberating and life changing, we can begin the process of finding out who we really are and what we really want out of this world and not what was decided for us. The world is your playground, make your own rules.

The Women Who Came Before Me:

I was always labeled a *Malcriada*.
A young girl way too loud,
With too many questions people did not have
    the answers to.
This made the men in my family tell a little girl,
How before, women like me were beaten.
How they would have made an example out of me,
For the world to see.
They did not see why this made me stronger,
And not afraid.
I knew then the privilege I had to be able to talk back,
As many before me were not granted this liberty.
Maybe this is why I was so loud,
Because I was speaking for all the women who
    came before me.
The ones who were silenced through violence.
So, I did what any little girl would.
I filled our living rooms with my words like rapid fire.
And each time, the curse got weaker.
I cast harry potter spells on sexist uncles,
And sent religious hypocrites to hell.
It was the power granted to me,
By all the women who did not have the chance.
The beauty in a family of fighters.
Women who made meals out of nothing,
Built homes from dust,
Sown together at the hips of trauma,
And healed together through prayer.
The power of our ancestors still protecting and guiding us.
Healing the generation before you,
Allows you to heal the ones who come after.
You are only one woman.

But the scariest part about a fire,
Is how fast it spreads,
And the trail it leaves.
This one is for the women who come after me.

Illustration by Jamcy Stephen Maquilon

CHAPTER 14
a Letter to The Little Sister I Never Had

As a woman, your intuition is one of the most powerful things you possess, and is one of the many things that gets stronger the more you use it. As young girls, it is easy to start getting older and begin to stray away from our internal answers, getting lost in the confusion while people try to fill your head with noise and what they think is best for you. I admit that when I was a young girl, I let people influence me and drive me off course, but now I give credit to the incredible people around me who dragged me back in by the ear, *por la buena o la mala*. It took hundreds of books, countless seminars, documentaries, articles, and conversations with women who have been through the same to learn from the mistake of allowing people to sway what I knew in my heart felt right. Now as a woman I can appreciate these frustrating moments that are teaching me the bigger picture. Even though we deal with many tough situations that only we can relate to, womanhood is one of the most beautiful things we get to experience. Sometimes it takes listening to others' advice over yourself, then watching things drastically fall apart before you can finally learn to stand your ground and listen to your gut. Women are born with this guide inside of them, but after many years of looking outside for answers or experiencing manipulation or trauma, they can lose their sense of touch with themselves. But it is never too late to get it back.

Women who have worked at building their internal map throughout the years walk a certain way; these women are almost never weak. They do not budge because they know what they want and what to do to get it; there is nobody they trust more than themselves, and there is nothing powerful enough to shake that foundation. I remember my mom always telling me, "*La que ve, no fracasa,*" which translate to "the one who watches does not get hurt." As a young girl, I loved to watch people, but more than anything I was an avid listener. I learned from peoples' past mistakes by listening to the tales of the present; I paid very close attention to everything and decided what I wanted my life to look like. I had the pleasure of being raised around many different kinds of women: ones who married young and had families, those who owned businesses, and those who were widowed, as well as many community church leaders. I had a favorite aunt whose dream was to become a salon owner; she was always known as the queen of "rolos," but her husband prohibited her because he was scared of the times she would be out of his sight as she was a very beautiful and charismatic woman. At 12, I knew two things: I did not want to give up my dreams in return for a happy husband, and I did not want the kind of husband who would dare ask me to. I picked and chose things I wanted and discarded what I did not. I knew that preparing for these things did not mean I would never trip or mess up; it just meant I would be able to pick myself up a little bit quicker because I know who I am and what I bring to this world. So even if you make mistakes, do not beat yourself up. The anger and sadness that comes when processing pain does not allow you to see past it in the moment, and that's all right. Take your time to feel the disappointment. Eventually you will be able to see the beauty in the lessons and allow others to learn from what you have been through. I spent many years diving into empowerment and self-awareness because I wanted to create a life for myself where I used the fire inside of me, while still remaining vulnerable and happy. I wanted to lead a life of love, respect, and honor for myself because I wanted to give this to the people around me. They deserved to have the best parts of me. I learned by paying attention to what I wanted my life to be like and what I would not accept outside of it.

<u>Below are a few things I decided were the boundaries I would create for my life. I want you to do the same for yours.</u>

- Get used to stopping people when they speak over you.
- Stop the negative talk. Treat yourself like your best friend with compassion and care.

- Never allow someone to have to tell you more than once they do not want you.
- Stop starting your questions with "I'm sorry."
- Do not allow people to mispronounce your name. No matter how many times you have to repeat yourself.
- Support and uplift great women in male-dominated spaces.
- This life is yours and nobody is going to rescue you.
- If it feels wrong, don't do it no matter who tries to tell you to.
- Confidence is more than liking your looks. Believe in what you do.
- To love yourself is to be incredibly honest. Adjust what needs work.
- Never lower your standards. Affirm what you want.
- Figure out your core values and never fold on them. Your self-respect will suffer greatly if you do.
- Speak up for what you want. Passiveness brings you disappointment.
- When your anger is valid, do not allow people to gaslight you.
- Listen to the concerns of the people who truly care about you. Always be your own filter. Some people love you, and some people are projecting.
- Choose yourself over the warmth of a body that does not respect you.

- Say no when you do not want to do something, even if you have to fight your guilt. (This is extremely important because of the next step.)
- When you do say yes, know that your word is your bond. Show up every time.
- Listen to understand, not to counter argue.
- In times of low confidence, let arrogance overpower your self-doubt. Adjust accordingly.
- Don't adapt to anything; bring your influence everywhere.
- Unlearn the chaos and reteach yourself peace.
- Follow your voice. Do not allow others to influence your decisions.
- Trends change every few months. Only do things for yourself.
- Leave those who disrespect your purpose. No questions asked.
- Never be so consumed in another person that you lose your soul.

To be a woman is to be bombarded with opinions, ideas, thoughts, and outside influences as to what is right for your life. This is why many women grow up to be extremely passive and look for guidance in outside sources. My main point is for women to be self-sufficient. This has nothing to do with you being incapable of developing your own thought process, but ultimately just not trusting yourself. When you have experienced noise for so many years and it finally gets quiet, you think the noise was normal and you keep searching for it. I wrote this as a short guideline for young women everywhere, for girls who might not have the best relationships with the women in their lives or who are just looking for some guidance. This one is for my little sisters around the world. I want you to lead your lives, to make sure the things you want come from your soul and not outside opinions, but remember that outsiders can be people you love with good intentions too. Our parents, family, and friends can mean well, and you can always be receptive to things your loved ones bring to you, but you have to make sure you take everything with a grain of salt and still make your decisions based on who you are and what you want. Be a woman who does things that makes herself happy, from small self-care routines to taking time away from a hectic days for yourself, meditating and celebrating your small wins. Get rid of people who bring you harm; set new boundaries in old relationships and complete small tasks that have been sitting in the back of your head to clear your mind. It means to demand respect even when your voice shakes and to build an abundant life outside of people, things, or relationships. To protect yourself and the great women around you. To stand up for yourself in a world that calls everything you do dramatic. I hope you know it will be so worth it to live a life you truly love when you lose the cover of insecurity and get what you deserve. Welcome home.

CHAPTER 15
Moving Forward:
Following The Fire

The first form of freedom is breaking the invisible chains wrapped around our necks by ego and fear. The beauty that comes after letting go of the misconceptions, thoughts, and doubts holding us hostage. This is the first form of true liberation. Believing in yourself, your art, and your people is the highest form of self-respect as well as knowing the honor it brings your ancestors to live a joyful life. I want you to understand that trauma can be generational and repetitive, so healing your wounds is an act of resistance in itself. To fight and get your soul back, so you can become what you were intended for this world. To learn emotional intelligence in our own lives so we can lead the next generation into a world from which they do not have to heal. Understanding that when you take care of yourself, the world thrives and so do our children. To protect and teach our youth so we can shield them the way we wish we had been. To give children who have been abused a voice and a home so they do not ever feel as if they were going through these things alone.

In Caribbean culture, we are taught to keep things in the vicinity of our four walls. They teach us that to find therapy and healing through outside sources is to invite strangers into your home and your family business. Do not believe this. Silence does not bring healing; it only allows people to have an excuse to ignore it. My wish is for you to leave everybody you come in contact with feeling better than they were before they met you. And for women to know they do not have to live a life of rules and accommodation for everyone around them but themselves. To not put time restrictions on when love or children should come into your life and to never create fairy tales with others in mind. I want you to look at your parents as people who are going through their own personal journeys and not just as our caregivers, so we can try to mend the important relationships in our life by being compassionate, yet still holding them accountable for the ways they have treated you.

I want Dominicans to act as a bridge for our island… to denounce racist and sexist rhetoric and to treat Haitians like our brothers and sisters. I want to remind young Dominicans and other Latinos everywhere who are anti-racism, sexism and capitalism, that holding our people accountable does not make you a "vende patria," but keeping silence does. I want women to be a lending voice to the ones who lack guidance or confidence. I hope you truly learn to deal with what you have gone through and not succumb to damaging vices like liquor, drugs, and sex to numb the pain. But I also want you know that even if you have, it is never too late to come home. I hope you know it isn't normal to be confined to one person and live in insecurity. I hope you have learned that you do not need to know how to navigate through chaos. I hope I brought awareness to a topic you did not know about and that you learned something you had not known prior to opening this book. I hope you were able to pinpoint an avenue you can work on and pass it along to the people in your life. I hope you were able to view yourself through the lens of honesty, no matter how uncomfortable it may have been. I hope you find your personal relationship with God and religion if this is what you want—and that what you were taught was not always necessarily right because the adults helping us were just as lost. I hope you know we all bring something to the table, and the key is to find your avenue and dominate. I hope you know every time you heal your wounds your ancestors rejoice. I hope you believe in yourself so much you chase the fire inside of you even if it burns.

It took me six years to finish this book, not because I was writing it for so long but because I was terrified of walking down unmarked territory. The fear of the unknown stops so many of us from doing the things we were placed on this earth for. May you chase the nervousness and butterflies that come with doing something new. The oppressor has spent centuries playing on our insecurities and self-doubt although our communities are the creators of culture and we make this world move. I hope you know how valuable you are and what you bring to this world. I hope you walk into every room with God like confidence. I hope you know if you have made it to the end of this book, I love you. Thank you for reading my brain. May you spend most of your time laughing so hard you need to gasp for air. May your foundation be so strong you just know this world is *so* much better with you in it. May you experience a love so pure you cannot help but to believe in the stars aligning and a joy so magical you forget pain exists for a moment. I hope you walk like your ancestors fought tooth and nail to simply exist, because they did. Let your purpose guide you and pass along important information as you go, as this allows us all to heal collectively. Remain you no matter what room you enter and like Mami always says: *Que Dios te acompañe. May God walk with you every step of the way.*

Five books you should read:

Darling You Can't Do Both by Janet Kestin & Nancy Vonk.
Feel The Fear & Do It Anyway by Susan Jeffers.
Gaslighting by Theresa J. Covert.
The Afro-Latino: A Historical Journey by Leslie K. Best.
Negotiating Respect by Brendan Jamal Thornton.

Contact the Author:

Instagram: LizbelOrtiz
Email: LizbelOrtiz@Hotmail.com